Learning Rust

A comprehensive guide to writing Rust applications

Paul Johnson
Vesa Kaihlavirta

BIRMINGHAM - MUMBAI

Learning Rust

First published: November 2017

Production reference: 1221117

Published by Packt Publishing Ltd.
Livery Place
35 Livery Street
Birmingham
B3 2PB, UK.
ISBN 978-1-78588-430-6

www.packtpub.com

Credits

Authors
Paul Johnson
Vesa Kaihlavirta

Reviewer
Ivo Balbaert

Commissioning Editor
Kunal Parikh

Acquisition Editor
Denim Pinto

Content Development Editor
Nikhil Borkar

Technical Editor
Madhunikita Sunil Chindarkar

Copy Editor
Safis Editing

Project Coordinator
Ulhas Kambali

Proofreader
Safis Editing

Indexer
Rekha Nair

Graphics
Kirk D'Penha

Production Coordinator
Arvindkumar Gupta

About the Authors

Paul Johnson has been writing software since the early 1980s on machines ranging from the ZX81 and servers to his trusty Mac, and has used more languages than he can remember. He is a qualified scuba diver and college lecturer. Paul lives with his wife, kids, and pets, and listens to an inordinate amount of rock and metal on Primordial Radio. This is his third book for Packt.

As has been pointed out to me by my wife, I'm older now than before. That's not to say that I've not learned things in that time. One of the more useful things I've learned is the Rust language. Life is about learning.

I've developed a number of server-side applications over the years, and hit many issues with memory management and ensuring safety across threads in an environment where other developers don't always understand the need for such things; it's been a nightmare. Rust simply removes these bad experiences.

This book could not have been written without my wife, Becki. She has taken up the slack when I've needed to work and not complained when, instead of sunning myself in Turkey on holiday, I've been away on other things, so only there in body. Her patience, love, companionship, and poking me are the reason why it's been done. Thanks, baby.

Willow, Ollie, George, Rich, Ash (as well as Lou and Angel) have not really helped, but I want to give them a mention, as no book I write would be complete without giving them a mention.

I need to thank the folks over at Packt who, throughout the writing of this book, have seen staff changes, numerous rewrites, and many other ups and downs, but all along have had a happy smile and encouraging word.

Here's to the next book, folks!

Credits

Authors
Paul Johnson
Vesa Kaihlavirta

Reviewer
Ivo Balbaert

Commissioning Editor
Kunal Parikh

Acquisition Editor
Denim Pinto

Content Development Editor
Nikhil Borkar

Technical Editor
Madhunikita Sunil Chindarkar

Copy Editor
Safis Editing

Project Coordinator
Ulhas Kambali

Proofreader
Safis Editing

Indexer
Rekha Nair

Graphics
Kirk D'Penha

Production Coordinator
Arvindkumar Gupta

About the Authors

Paul Johnson has been writing software since the early 1980s on machines ranging from the ZX81 and servers to his trusty Mac, and has used more languages than he can remember. He is a qualified scuba diver and college lecturer. Paul lives with his wife, kids, and pets, and listens to an inordinate amount of rock and metal on Primordial Radio. This is his third book for Packt.

As has been pointed out to me by my wife, I'm older now than before. That's not to say that I've not learned things in that time. One of the more useful things I've learned is the Rust language. Life is about learning.

I've developed a number of server-side applications over the years, and hit many issues with memory management and ensuring safety across threads in an environment where other developers don't always understand the need for such things; it's been a nightmare. Rust simply removes these bad experiences.

This book could not have been written without my wife, Becki. She has taken up the slack when I've needed to work and not complained when, instead of sunning myself in Turkey on holiday, I've been away on other things, so only there in body. Her patience, love, companionship, and poking me are the reason why it's been done. Thanks, baby.

Willow, Ollie, George, Rich, Ash (as well as Lou and Angel) have not really helped, but I want to give them a mention, as no book I write would be complete without giving them a mention.

I need to thank the folks over at Packt who, throughout the writing of this book, have seen staff changes, numerous rewrites, and many other ups and downs, but all along have had a happy smile and encouraging word.

Here's to the next book, folks!

Vesa Kaihlavirta has been programming since he was 5, beginning with C64 Basic. His main professional goal in life is to increase awareness about programming languages and software quality in all industries that use software. He's an Arch Linux Developer Fellow and has been working in the telecom and financial industry for over a decade. Vesa lives in Central Finland, in Jyväskylä. Vesa worked on the final editing phase of *Learning Rust*.

About the Reviewer

Ivo Balbaert is currently a lecturer of (web) programming and databases at CVO Antwerpen (www.cvoantwerpen.be), a community college in Belgium. He received a PhD in applied physics from the University of Antwerp in 1986. He worked for 20 years in the software industry as a developer and consultant at several companies, and for 10 years as a project manager at the Antwerp University Hospital. From 2000 onwards, he switched to partly teaching and partly developing software (KHM Mechelen, CVO Antwerpen).

In 2012, he authored a book on the Go programming language, *The Way To Go*, IUniverse. In 2013, in collaboration with Dzenan Ridzanovic, he wrote *Learning Dart* and *Dart Cookbook*, followed by *Getting Started with Julia Programming Language* and *Rust Essentials*, all published by Packt.

www.PacktPub.com

For support files and downloads related to your book, please visit www.PacktPub.com. Did you know that Packt offers eBook versions of every book published, with PDF and ePub files available? You can upgrade to the eBook version at www.PacktPub.com and as a print book customer, you are entitled to a discount on the eBook copy. Get in touch with us at service@packtpub.com for more details. At www.PacktPub.com, you can also read a collection of free technical articles, sign up for a range of free newsletters and receive exclusive discounts and offers on Packt books and eBooks.

https://www.packtpub.com/mapt

Get the most in-demand software skills with Mapt. Mapt gives you full access to all Packt books and video courses, as well as industry-leading tools to help you plan your personal development and advance your career.

Why subscribe?

- Fully searchable across every book published by Packt
- Copy and paste, print, and bookmark content
- On demand and accessible via a web browser

Customer Feedback

Thanks for purchasing this Packt book. At Packt, quality is at the heart of our editorial process. To help us improve, please leave us an honest review on this book's Amazon page at `https://www.amazon.com/dp/1785884301`.

If you'd like to join our team of regular reviewers, you can email us at `customerreviews@packtpub.com`. We award our regular reviewers with free eBooks and videos in exchange for their valuable feedback. Help us be relentless in improving our products!

Table of Contents

Preface

Rust is a new programming language. It offers performance and safety that is equivalent to, or even surpasses, modern C++ while being a modern language with a relatively low barrier to entry. Rust's momentum, combined with its active and friendly community, promise a great future for the language.

While modern and fluent, Rust is not a particularly easy language. The memory management system keeps track of the life of every entity that is used in your program and is designed in such a way that this tracking can typically happen entirely at compile time. The Rust programmer's burden is to help the compiler when it cannot decide for itself what should happen. Since modern programming is possible without ever facing such responsibilities, a modern programmer may not immediately feel comfortable with Rust.

However, like all expertise and skill, the more difficult it is to attain, the more valuable it is, and this book is here to help you. This book covers the basics of Rust, enabling you to gain enough skills to start programming with it.

What this book covers

Chapter 1, *Introducing and Installing Rust*, deals with installing the Rust toolset and using the basic tools.

Chapter 2, *Variables*, focuses on using different kinds of variables.

Chapter 3, *Input and Output*, covers the basic I/O.

Chapter 4, *Conditions, Recursion, and Loops*, goes through the different loops and iterative methods of Rust.

Chapter 5, *Remember, Remember*, covers Rust's memory handling system.

Chapter 6, *Creating Your Own Rust Applications*, gives you the task of building a complete Rust application.

Chapter 7, *Matching and Structures*, teaches you compound data types and how to destructure them.

Chapter 8, *The Rust Application Lifetime*, covers Rust's unique ownership, borrowing, and lifetime system, which enables resource safety without garbage collection.

Chapter 9, *Introducing Generics, Impl, and Traits*, goes through Rust's generic types.

Chapter 10, *Creating Your Own Crate*, instructs you how to build your own contained packages of Rust code.

Chapter 11, *Concurrency in Rust*, looks at concurrency and parallelism techniques.

Chapter 12, *Now It's Your Turn!*, gives you another set of tasks to complete.

Chapter 13, *The Standard Library*, covers Rust's standard library.

Chapter 14, *Foreign Function Interfaces*, introduces techniques to interface Rust code with C programs.

What you need for this book

To really dive into the content of this book, you should write out the example code and do the exercises. For that, you'll need a fairly recent computer; a gigabyte of RAM should be enough for the purposes of this book, but the more you have the faster the builds will be.

Linux is the best supported operating system here, but Rust itself is a first-class citizen on macOS and recent versions of Windows, so all the examples should adapt well there.

Who this book is for

This book will appeal to application developers who would like to build applications with Rust. No knowledge of programming is required.

Conventions

In this book, you will find a number of text styles that distinguish between different kinds of information. Here are some examples of these styles and an explanation of their meaning. Code words in text, database table names, folder names, filenames, file extensions, pathnames, dummy URLs, user input, and Twitter handles are shown as follows: "A shorter form is available in the unwrap method. This is the same as the expect method, but it doesn't print out anything in case of a failure."

A block of code is set as follows:

```
let mut file = File::create("myxml_file.xml").unwrap();
let mut output = io::stdout();
let mut input = io::stdin();
```

Any command-line input or output is written as follows:

```
cd app_name
cargo build app_name
```

New terms and **important words** are shown in bold. Words that you see on the screen, for example, in menus or dialog boxes, appear in the text like this: "Open up **Visual Studio Code** and go to the Command Palette, either by the **View** menu or by the keyboard shortcut *Ctrl + Shift + P* (which may differ between platforms)."

Warnings or important notes appear like this.

Tips and tricks appear like this.

Reader feedback

Feedback from our readers is always welcome. Let us know what you think about this book-what you liked or disliked. Reader feedback is important for us as it helps us develop titles that you will really get the most out of. To send us general feedback, simply email feedback@packtpub.com, and mention the book's title in the subject of your message. If there is a topic that you have expertise in and you are interested in either writing or contributing to a book, see our author guide at www.packtpub.com/authors.

Customer support

Now that you are the proud owner of a Packt book, we have a number of things to help you to get the most from your purchase.

Downloading the example code

You can download the example code files for this book from your account at `http://www.packtpub.com`. If you purchased this book elsewhere, you can visit `http://www.packtpub.com/support` and register to have the files emailed directly to you. You can download the code files by following these steps:

1. Log in or register to our website using your email address and password.
2. Hover the mouse pointer on the **SUPPORT** tab at the top.
3. Click on **Code Downloads & Errata**.
4. Enter the name of the book in the **Search** box.
5. Select the book for which you're looking to download the code files.
6. Choose from the drop-down menu where you purchased this book from.
7. Click on **Code Download**.

Once the file is downloaded, please make sure that you unzip or extract the folder using the latest version of:

- WinRAR / 7-Zip for Windows
- Zipeg / iZip / UnRarX for Mac
- 7-Zip / PeaZip for Linux

The code bundle for the book is also hosted on GitHub at `https://github.com/PacktPublishing/Learning-Rust`. We also have other code bundles from our rich catalog of books and videos available at `https://github.com/PacktPublishing/`. Check them out!

Errata

Although we have taken every care to ensure the accuracy of our content, mistakes do happen. If you find a mistake in one of our books-maybe a mistake in the text or the code-we would be grateful if you could report this to us. By doing so, you can save other readers from frustration and help us improve subsequent versions of this book. If you find any errata, please report them by visiting `http://www.packtpub.com/submit-errata`, selecting your book, clicking on the **Errata Submission Form** link, and entering the details of your errata. Once your errata are verified, your submission will be accepted and the errata will be uploaded to our website or added to any list of existing errata under the Errata section of that title. To view the previously submitted errata, go to `https://www.packtpub.com/books/content/support` and enter the name of the book in the search field. The required information will appear under the **Errata** section.

Piracy

Piracy of copyrighted material on the internet is an ongoing problem across all media. At Packt, we take the protection of our copyright and licenses very seriously. If you come across any illegal copies of our works in any form on the internet, please provide us with the location address or website name immediately so that we can pursue a remedy. Please contact us at `copyright@packtpub.com` with a link to the suspected pirated material. We appreciate your help in protecting our authors and our ability to bring you valuable content.

Questions

If you have a problem with any aspect of this book, you can contact us at `questions@packtpub.com`, and we will do our best to address the problem.

1

Introducing and Installing Rust

Rust is a fairly new addition to the ever-growing number of programming languages available to developers. If you've never used Rust, but come from pretty much any procedural language (such as C or Pascal) or are used to shell scripting, then you should very quickly feel right at home when using Rust.

Getting to grips with Rust is simple enough, and in this chapter we will cover the following topics:

- Installing Rust with rustup
- Testing the installation
- Setting up a project
- Looking at the IDEs available
- Automation using Cargo

Installing Rust

As with most languages, Rust is available for a wide number of platforms. It would be impossible to go through installing the compiler on every variant of every operating system. Fortunately, there's an official method of installing Rust, and even though the details may differ slightly, the process is almost the same on all platforms. Therefore, this book will cover installing Rust using rustup on Fedora 27.

`https://rustup.rs` always contains up-to-date instructions on how to get going on all platforms. On Linux and macOS, it will look something like this:

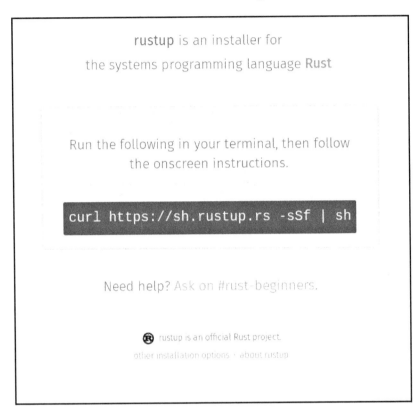

On Windows, this text is replaced by a link to `rustup-init.exe`, which is an executable that installs and sets up rustup on Windows.

Installing rustup on Linux

Run the suggested command that is shown at `https://rustup.rs`. Run this command in a Terminal. The script suggests some defaults and asks you to confirm them. This is roughly what it should look like after completing the whole script:

```
                                    Terminal                                    ⊗

[pfj@localhost]$ curl https://sh.rustup.rs -sSf | sh
info: downloading installer

Welcome to Rust!

This will download and install the official compiler for the Rust programming
language, and its package manager, Cargo.

It will add the cargo, rustc, rustup and other commands to Cargo's bin
directory, located at:

  /home/pfj/.cargo/bin

This path will then be added to your PATH environment variable by modifying the
profile files located at:

  /home/pfj/.profile
  /home/pfj/.bash_profile

You can uninstall at any time with rustup self uninstall and these changes will
be reverted.

Current installation options:

    default host triple: x86_64-unknown-linux-gnu
      default toolchain: stable
  modify PATH variable: yes

1) Proceed with installation (default)
2) Customize installation
3) Cancel installation
1

info: syncing channel updates for 'stable-x86_64-unknown-linux-gnu'
info: latest update on 2017-10-12, rust version 1.21.0 (3b72af97e 2017-10-09)
info: downloading component 'rustc'
 38.5 MiB /  38.5 MiB (100 %) 476.8 KiB/s ETA:    0 s
info: downloading component 'rust-std'
 56.7 MiB /  56.7 MiB (100 %) 940.8 KiB/s ETA:    0 s
info: downloading component 'cargo'
  3.7 MiB /   3.7 MiB (100 %) 863.8 KiB/s ETA:    0 s
info: downloading component 'rust-docs'
  4.1 MiB /   4.1 MiB (100 %) 739.0 KiB/s ETA:    0 s
info: installing component 'rustc'
info: installing component 'rust-std'
info: installing component 'cargo'
info: installing component 'rust-docs'
info: default toolchain set to 'stable'

  stable installed - rustc 1.21.0 (3b72af97e 2017-10-09)


Rust is installed now. Great!

To get started you need Cargo's bin directory ($HOME/.cargo/bin) in your PATH
environment variable. Next time you log in this will be done automatically.

To configure your current shell run source $HOME/.cargo/env
[pfj@localhost]$
```

Note that this script attempts to set up rustup for your user by editing your `.profile` and `.bash_profile` files. If you are using a custom setup, such as another shell, you may need to add the `source $HOME/.cargo/env` command manually.

After finishing this script, you can verify that it worked by logging off and on from your Terminal and verifying that the tools are in your path:

gcc prerequisites

To build any software that links against external libraries, you will need a C compiler and development versions of any libraries you may be linking against. To ensure that things work properly, install the compiler using the standard method for your operating system.

In Fedora, this would be done using the dnf tool:

```
sudo dnf install -y gcc
```

If you are unsure whether you have gcc installed, type the following command in a terminal window:

```
gcc --version
```

If gcc is installed, you'll see something like this:

Testing your installation

Open a command-prompt window and type this:

```
rustc --version
```

If everything was installed correctly, you will see something like this:

Integrated Development Environment

To effectively code Rust, you will need at least some sort of text editor. All popular editors are properly supported, so if your favorite is Vim, Emacs, or any of the others, you will find a high-quality Rust extension there. The website `https://areweideyet.com/` should give a current view of how things are.

We will cover the lightweight IDE from Microsoft, **Visual Studio Code**, and its most current Rust extension, called simply **Rust**. This IDE should work fairly well in all the different desktop environments. Installation instructions and packages for several platforms are available at Visual Studio Code's main site, `https://code.visualstudio.com`.

1. Open up **Visual Studio Code** and go to the Command Palette, either by the **View** menu or by the keyboard shortcut *Ctrl + Shift + P* (which may differ between platforms). Type in `install extension` to look for the proper command, and then select **Install Extensions**:

2. After selecting this, type `rust` into the next field to look for the **Rust** extension. At the time of writing, the most recent one is made by **kalitaalexey**:

3. You can install Rust right away by pressing **Install**; alternatively, click on the list item itself to show information about the extension first. After installing it, reload the editor. The **Rust** extension is now installed and ready to use!

Your first Rust project

Your first Rust project is not going to be particularly amazing. If anything, it's going to serve four purposes:

- Showing the structure of a Rust project
- Showing how to create a project by hand
- Showing how to create a project using the Rust Cargo script
- Compiling and executing the program

Structure of a Rust project

A Rust project (irrespective of the platform you are developing on) will have the following structure:

```
Pauls-iMac:firstproject PFJ$ tree .
.
├── Cargo.toml
└── src
    └── main.rs
```

The preceding screenshot shows the structure of the simplest Rust project, and as such can be replicated using the following commands:

OS X/Linux	Windows (from the command prompt)
`mkdir firstproject cd firstproject touch Cargo.toml mkdir src cd src touch main.rs`	`md firstproject cd firstproject md src echo $null >> Cargo.toml cd src echo $null >> main.rs`

The `echo $null >> filename` command creates an empty file without the need to start Notepad; save the file and exit.

The `Cargo.toml` file is the Rust equivalent of a **Makefile**. When the `.toml` file is created by hand, it should be edited to contain something like this:

```
[package]
name = "firstproject"
version = "0.1.0"
authors = ["Paul Johnson <paul@snuberry-software.co.uk>"]
```

The structure of a Rust project can expand to include documentation as well as the build structure, as follows:

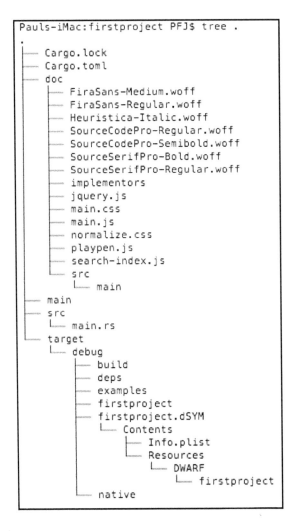

```
Pauls-iMac:firstproject PFJ$ tree .
.
├── Cargo.lock
├── Cargo.toml
├── doc
│   ├── FiraSans-Medium.woff
│   ├── FiraSans-Regular.woff
│   ├── Heuristica-Italic.woff
│   ├── SourceCodePro-Regular.woff
│   ├── SourceCodePro-Semibold.woff
│   ├── SourceSerifPro-Bold.woff
│   ├── SourceSerifPro-Regular.woff
│   ├── implementors
│   ├── jquery.js
│   ├── main.css
│   ├── main.js
│   ├── normalize.css
│   ├── playpen.js
│   ├── search-index.js
│   └── src
│       └── main
├── main
├── src
│   └── main.rs
└── target
    └── debug
        ├── build
        ├── deps
        ├── examples
        ├── firstproject
        ├── firstproject.dSYM
        │   └── Contents
        │       ├── Info.plist
        │       └── Resources
        │           └── DWARF
        │               └── firstproject
        └── native
```

Automating things

While there is nothing wrong with creating a Rust project by hand, Rust does come with a very handy utility called **Cargo**. Cargo can be used not only to automate the setting up of a project, but also to compile and execute Rust code. Cargo can be used to create the parts required for a library instead of an executable, and can also generate application documentation.

Creating a binary package using Cargo

As with any other script, Cargo works (by default) on the current working directory. (For example, while writing this chapter, my working directory for the example code is `~/Developer/Rust/chapter0` on the Mac and Linux boxes, and `J:\Developer\Rust\Chapter0` on the Windows 10 machine.)

In its simplest form, Cargo can generate the correct file structure like this:

```
cargo new demo_app_name -bin
```

The preceding command tells Cargo to create a new structure called `demo_app_name`, and that it is to be a binary. If you remove `-bin`, it creates a structure called, which is going to be a library (or more accurately, something other than a binary).

If you don't wish to use the root (say you want to create a library within your binary framework), then instead of `demo_app_name`, you append the structure before the name relating to your working directory.

In the small example I gave earlier, if I wanted to create a library within my binary structure, I would use the following:

```
cargo new app_name/mylib
```

That will create a structure like this:

```
Pauls-MacBook-Pro:chapter0 PFJ$ tree demo_app_name
demo_app_name
├── Cargo.toml
├── mylib
│   ├── Cargo.toml
│   └── src
│       └── lib.rs
└── src
    └── main.rs
```

The `Cargo.toml` file requires no editing (at this stage), as it contains the information we had to enter manually when we created the project by hand.

 Cargo has a number of directory separator *translators*. This means that the preceding example can be used on OS X, Linux, and Windows without an issue; Cargo has converted the / to \ for Windows.

Using Cargo to build and run an application

As we are all able to create directory structures, Cargo is then able to build and execute our source code.

If you look at the source code that comes with this chapter, you will find a directory called `app_name`. To build this package using Cargo, type the following from a Terminal (or command on Windows) window:

```
cd app_name
cargo build app_name
```

This will build the source code; finally you will be informed that the compilation has been successful:

```
Pauls-MacBook-Pro:chapter0 PFJ$ cd app_name
Pauls-MacBook-Pro:app_name PFJ$ cargo build
   Compiling app_name v0.1.0 (file:///Users/PFJ/Developer/rust/chapter0/app_name)
```

Next, we can use Cargo to execute the binary as follows:

```
cargo run
```

If everything has worked, you will see something like the following:

```
Pauls-MacBook-Pro:app_name PFJ$ cargo run
     Running `target/debug/app_name`
Hello, world!
```

As with any sort of utility, it's possible to "daisy-chain" the build and execution into one line, as follows:

```
cargo build; cargo run
```

 You may be wondering why the first operation performed was to move into the application structure rather than just type `cargo build`. This is because Cargo is looking for the `Cargo.toml` file (remember, this acts as a build script).

Cleaning your source tree with Cargo

When the Rust compiler compiles the source files, it generates something known as an object file. The object file takes the source file (which we can read and understand) and compiles this into a form that can be joined with other libraries to create a binary.

This is a good idea, as it cuts down on compilation time; if a source file has not been changed, there is no need to recompile the file, as the object file will be the same.

Sometimes, the object file becomes out of date, or code in another object file causes a panic due to conflicts. In this case, it is not uncommon to "clean" the build. This removes the object files, and the compiler then has to recompile all the source files.

Also, it should always be performed prior to creating a release build.

The standard Unix `make` program performs this with the `clean` command (`make clean`). Cargo performs the clean operation in a way similar to the `make` utility in Unix:

```
cargo clean
```

A comparison of the directories shows what happens when using the preceding Cargo command:

```
.
├── Cargo.lock
├── Cargo.toml
├── src
│   └── main.rs
└── target
    └── debug
        ├── app_name
        ├── app_name.dSYM
        │   └── Contents
        │       ├── Info.plist
        │       └── Resources
        │           └── DWARF
        │               └── app_name
        ├── build
        ├── deps
        ├── examples
        └── native

11 directories, 6 files
Pauls-MacBook-Pro:app_name PFJ$ cargo clean
Pauls-MacBook-Pro:app_name PFJ$ tree
.
├── Cargo.lock
├── Cargo.toml
└── src
    └── main.rs
```

The entire target directory structure has simply been removed (the preceding screenshot was from a Mac, hence the dSYM and plist files. These do not exist on Linux and Windows).

Creating documentation using Cargo

As with other languages, Rust is able to create documentation based on meta tags with the source files. Take the following example:

```
fn main()
{
    print_multiply(4, 5);
}
```

```
/// A simple function example
///
/// # Examples
///
/// ```
/// print_multiply(3, 5);
///
/// ```

fn print_multiply(x: i32, y: i32)
{
    println!("x * y = {}", x * y);
}
```

The comments preceded by /// will be converted into documentation.

The documentation can be created in one of two ways: via Cargo or by using the **rustdoc** program.

rustdoc versus Cargo

As with the other operations provided by Cargo, when documentation is created, it acts as a wrapper for rustdoc. The only difference is that with rustdoc you have to specify the directory that the source file sits in. Cargo acts dumb in this case, and creates the documentation for all source files.

In its simplest form, the rustdoc command is used as follows:

```
cargo doc
rustdoc src/main.rs
```

Cargo does have the advantage of creating the doc structure within the root folder, whereas rustdoc creates the structure within the target (which is removed with cargo clean).

Using Cargo to help with your unit testing

Hopefully, unit testing is not something you will be unfamiliar with. A unit test is a test that operates on a specific function or method rather than an entire class or namespace. It ensures that the function operates correctly on the data it is presented with.

Unit tests within Rust are very simple to create (two examples are given in the `assert_unittest` and `unittest` directories). The following has been taken from the `unittest` example:

```
fn main() {
    println!("Tests have not been compiled, use rustc --test instead (or
cargo test)");
}

#[test]
fn multiply_test()
{
    if 2 * 3 == 5
    {
        println!("The multiply worked");
    }
}
```

When this is built and executed, you may be surprised by the following result:

```
Pauls-MacBook-Pro:unittest PFJ$ cargo test; cargo run
    Compiling unittest v0.1.0 (file:///Users/PFJ/Developer/rust/chapter0/unittest
)
src/main.rs:1:1: 3:2          function is never used: `main`, #[warn(dead_code)]
  on by default
src/main.rs:1 fn main() {
src/main.rs:2     println!("Tests have not been compiled, use rustc --test inste
ad");
src/main.rs:3 }
    Running target/debug/unittest-4970c5e6c17d9ffb

running 1 test
test multiply_test ... ok

test result: ok. 1 passed; 0 failed; 0 ignored; 0 measured
```

 The reason why this unit test has passed despite *2 x 3* not being *5* is because the unit test is not testing the result of the operation, but that the operation itself is working. It is very important that this distinction is understood from an early stage to prevent confusion later.

We have hit a limitation of unit testing: if we are not testing the data but the operation, how can we know that the result itself is correct?

Assert yourself!

Unit testing provides the developer with a number of methods called assertion methods:

```
#[test]
fn multiply()
{
    assert_eq!(5, 2 * 3);
}
```

In the preceding code snippet, we use the `assert_eq!` (assert equal) macro. The first argument is the answer expected, and the second argument is what is being tested. If *2 * 3 = 5*, then the assertion is true and passes the unit test.

Is there anything Cargo can't do?

For a Rust developer, Cargo is an amazing utility. In addition to these common facilities, it also has other commands, which are listed in the table that follows. All commands follow this form:

```
cargo <command> <opts>
```

Command	What it does
`fetch`	This command fetches the dependencies of a package from the network. If a lockfile is available, this command will ensure that all of the Git dependencies and/or registry dependencies are downloaded and locally available. The network is never called after a `cargo fetch` unless the lockfile changes. If the lockfile is not available, then this is the equivalent of `cargo generate-lockfile`. A lockfile is generated and all the dependencies are also updated.
`generate-lockfile`	This command generates the lockfile for a project. The lockfile is typically generated when `cargo build` is issued (you will see it as `Cargo.lockfile` in the directory structure).
`git-checkout`	This command checks out a Git repository. You will need to use it in the following form: `cargo git-checkout –url=URL`
`locate-project`	This command locates a package.

`login`	This command saves an API token from the registry locally. The call is in the following form: `cargo login –host=HOST    token`
`owner`	This command manages the owners of a crate on the registry. This allows the ownership of a crate (a crate is a Rust library) to be altered (`--add LOGIN` or `-remove LOGIN`) as well as adding tokens to the crate. This command will modify the owners for a package on the specified registry (or the default). Note that the owners of a package can upload new versions, yank old versions, and also modify the set of owners, so be cautious!
`package`	This command assembles the local package into a distributable tarball.
`pkgid`	This command prints a fully qualified package specification.
`publish`	This command uploads a package to the registry.
`read-manifest`	This command reads the manifest file (`.toml`).
`rustc`	This command compiles the complete package. The specified target for the current package will be compiled along with all of its dependencies. The specified options will all be passed to the final compiler invocation, not any of the dependencies. Note that the compiler will still unconditionally receive arguments such as `-L`, `--extern`, and `--crate-type`, and the specified options will simply be added to the compiler invocation. This command requires that only one target is being compiled. If more than one target is available for the current package, the filters `--lib`, `--bin`, and so on—must be used to select which target is compiled.
`search`	This command searches for packages at `https://crates.io/`.

update	This command updates dependencies as recorded in the local lockfile.
	Typical options are:
	• --package SPEC (package to update)
	• --aggressive (forcibly update all dependencies of <name> as well)
	• --precise PRECISE (update a single dependency to exactly PRECISE)
	This command requires that a Cargo.lock file already exists as generated by cargo build or related commands.
	If a package spec name (SPEC) is given, then a conservative update of the lockfile will be performed. This means that only the dependency specified by SPEC will be updated. Its transitive dependencies will be updated only if SPEC cannot be updated without updating the dependencies. All other dependencies will remain locked at their currently recorded versions.
	If PRECISE is specified, then --aggressive must not also be specified. The argument PRECISE is a string representing a precise revision that the package being updated should be updated to. For example, if the package comes from a Git repository, then PRECISE would be the exact revision that the repository should be updated to. If SPEC is not given, then all the dependencies will be re-resolved and updated.
verify-project	This command ensures that the project is correctly created.
version	This command shows the version of Cargo.
yank	This command removes a pushed crate from the index.
	The yank command removes a previously pushed crate version from the server's index. This command does not delete any data, and the crate will still be available for download via the registry's download link.
	Note that existing crates locked to a yanked version will still be able to download the yanked version to use it. Cargo will, however, not allow any new crates to be locked to any yanked version.

As you can now appreciate, the Cargo utility script is extremely powerful and flexible.

Summary

We now have a fully working installation of Rust, and are ready for the get-go. We've explained how to set up a project, both manually and via the Cargo utility, and you should already have an appreciation of how useful Cargo is.

In the next chapter, we'll be looking at the foundation of any language: **variables**.

2
Variables

As with all programming languages, we need a way to store information within our application. This information can be anything and, as with every other language, it's stored in a variable. However, unlike every other language, Rust does not store data in the same way as (say) C does.

To that end, in this chapter we will do the following:

- Understand variable mutability
- See how Rust stores information in a variable, and the types of variable available
- See how Rust deals with vector variable types
- Understand how Rust can and cannot manipulate variables
- See how Rust can pass variables
- Take a look at how Rust stores a variable internally

Variable mutability

Unlike many other languages, Rust defaults to non-mutability of variables. That means that variable bindings are actually constants if not explicitly defined as mutable. The compiler checks against all variable mutations and refuses to accept mutating non-mutable variable bindings.

 If you come from one of the C family of languages, a non-mutable can be considered to be roughly the same as a `const` type.

Creating a variable

To create a new variable binding in Rust, we use the following form:

```
let x = 1;
```

This means that we create a new variable binding called x whose content will be 1. The default type for numbers depends on the situation a bit, but usually it's a 32-bit signed integer. If we need a variable that can change, we use this form:

```
let mut x = 1;
```

By default, all variables in Rust are non-mutable; therefore, we have to explicitly define a variable as being mutable.

How can we tell the compiler that we want x to be an int?

Rust has a way of informing both the compiler and the developer of the variable type. For example, for a 32-bit int, we would use the following:

```
let x = 1i32;
```

In other words, x = 1, a 32-bit signed int.

If a variable is defined without the i32 (or any other value), the compiler will decide the type depending on how the value is used, defaulting to i32.

Defining other variable types

Other variable types can be declared in the same way as int variables.

Float

Much as with other languages, floating point arithmetic can be performed in Rust. As with an integer variable, a floating point variable is defined for a 32-bit float as follows:

```
let pi = 3.14f32;
```

For a 64-bit `float`, it will be defined as this:

```
let pi = 3.14f64;
```

The variables are literal values. Another way to declare the size would be via types:

```
let pi: f32 = 3.14;
```

 If a type is omitted (for example, let x = 3.14), the variable will be declared as a 64-bit floating point variable.

Signed and unsigned integers

A signed `int` (one that can have positive or negative values) is defined like this:

```
let sint = 10i32;
```

An unsigned `int` has a u instead of i in the definition:

```
let usint = 10u32;
```

Again, these are number literals, and the same declaration can be made via types:

```
let sint: i32 = 10;
```

 Both signed and unsigned `int` values can be 8, 16, 32, or 64-bits long.

Const and static

Rust has two types of constants: **consts** and **statics**. Consts are sort of like aliases: their contents are sort of replaced on the place where they are used. The syntax is like this:

```
const PI: f32 = 3.1415927;
```

Statics are more like variables. They have a global scope of the program, and are defined as follows:

```
static MY_VARIABLE: i32 = 255;
```

They cannot be altered.

Rust is able to guess the types of local function variables. This is called **local type inference**. However, it is only local, so types of statics and consts must always be typed out.

Defining the variable value before use

While it is not enforced in some languages, a variable must have an initial value in Rust, even if it is zero. This is good practice, and also helps when it comes to debugging since all variables have known contents. If they didn't, there'd be a risk of undefined behavior.

 Undefined behavior means that what the program does is anyone's guess. For instance, if variables did not have initial values, their values would be whatever happens to be in memory at the time that the value is allocated.

Strings

Typically, a string can be defined in one of two ways:

```
let myName = "my name";
```

This is known as a **string slice**. These will be dealt with in a while.

The second way is to use `String::new();`. This is a String, with a capital S. It is allocated in the heap and can grow dynamically.

At this point, it would be a good idea to break with the current narrative and discuss how Rust uses memory, as it will help greatly with explaining a number of upcoming topics.

How Rust uses memory

The memory occupied by any Rust program is split into two distinct areas: the heap and the stack. Simply put, the stack contains primitive variables, while the heap stores complex types. As with the mess on my daughter's bedroom floor, a heap can grow and grow until the available memory is exhausted. The stack is faster and simpler but may not grow without limits. Every binding in Rust is in a stack, but those bindings may refer to things in the heap, and elsewhere.

This all relates directly to the string example. The binding myName is in the stack, and refers to a literal static string, *my name*. That string being static means that it is somewhere in memory when the program starts. Its being static also means that it cannot be changed.

String::new, on the other hand, creates a String in the heap. It is initially empty, but may grow to fill the whole virtual memory space.

Here is an example of a growing String:

```
let mut myStringOne = "This is my first string ".to_owned();
let myStringTwo = "This is my second string. ";
let myStringThree = "This is my final string";
myStringOne = myStringOne + myStringTwo + myStringTwo + myStringThree +
myStringTwo;
```

One of the ways of creating Strings is to call the to_owned method on a string slice, like we have just done. There are other ways, but this is the most recommended one because it underlines the ownership issue. We'll get back to that later.

Here, the binding myStringOne starts out at 24 characters long, and would be allocated at least that size on the heap. The binding myStringOne is actually a reference to the position on the heap where myStringOne lives.

As we add to myStringOne, the size it occupies on the heap increases; however, the reference to the base position remains the same.

> The lifetime and scope of a variable have to be taken into account. For example, if we define a string within part of a function, and then try and access the string outside the function, we get a compiler error.

Back to Strings

As we saw before diverting onto the heap and stack, we can also define a string like this:

```
let mut myString = String::new();
```

The String:: tells the compiler that we are going to use the standard library, String, and we tell the program that we are going to create a mutable String and store a reference to it on the stack in something called myString.

The dynamic string can be created as either being empty, or with memory preallocated to it. For example, say we want to store the words *You'll never walk alone* (a total of 23 bytes), preallocating the space for them. This is how to do it:

```
let mut ynwa = String::with_capacity(23);
ynwa.push_str("You'll never walk alone");
```

This is just a performance optimization and is not typically required, since Strings grow automatically when they need to. The following does roughly the same job:

```
let mut ynwa = "You'll never walk alone".to_owned();
```

 Rust strings are not null-terminated, and consist entirely of valid Unicode. Therefore, they can contain null bytes and characters from any language, but they may require more bytes than they contain characters.

String slices

String slices can be confusing at first sight. We define a string slice like this:

```
let homeTeam = "Liverpool";
```

Coming from more dynamic languages, you might think that we are assigning the string `Liverpool` to the variable binding `homeTeam`. That's not exactly what happens, however. The `homeTeam` binding is actually a string slice: a reference to a part of the string that actually resides somewhere else.

The string slice is also not mutable.

The following will not work in Rust:

```
let homeTeam = "Liverpool";
let result = " beat ";
let awayTeam = "Manchester United";
let theString = homeTeam + result + awayTeam;
```

The compiler will not allow this, and will give an error as follows:

```
Pauls-MacBook-Pro:addstring-1 PFJ$ cargo build
   Compiling addstring-1 v0.1.0 (file:///Users/PFJ/Developer/rust/chapter1/addstring-1)
src/main.rs:6:20: 6:28 error: binary operation `+` cannot be applied to type `&str` [E0369]
src/main.rs:6     let fullLine = homeTeam + result + awayTeam;
                  ^~~~~~~~~~~~~~
error: aborting due to previous error
Could not compile `addstring-1`.
```

We cannot concatenate the slice directly, since string slices cannot be mutable. To do that, we need to first convert the string slice into something that is mutable, or build the string with something like the `format!` macro. Let's try them both.

Like before, the `to_owned()` method takes the slice the method is attached to, and converts it to a `String` type:

```
fn main() {
    let homeTeam = "Liverpool";
    let result = " beat ";
    let awayTeam = "Manchester United";
    let fullLine = homeTeam.to_owned() + result + awayTeam;
    println!("{}", fullLine);
}
```

The `to_owned()` method is only applied to the first slice. This converts the string slice `homeTeam` into a String, and using the + operator on a String is fine.

When this is built and executed, you will see the following:

```
Pauls-MacBook-Pro:addstring-2 PFJ$ cargo build
   Compiling addstring-2 v0.1.0 (file:///Users/PFJ/Developer/rust/chapter1/addstring-2)
src/main.rs:2:6: 2:14          variable `homeTeam` should have a snake case name such as `ho
me_team`, #[warn(non_snake_case)] on by default
src/main.rs:2    let homeTeam = "Liverpool";

src/main.rs:4:9: 4:17          variable `awayTeam` should have a snake case name such as `aw
ay_team`, #[warn(non_snake_case)] on by default
src/main.rs:4     let awayTeam = "Manchester United";

src/main.rs:6:9: 6:17          variable `fullLine` should have a snake case name such as `fu
ll_line`, #[warn(non_snake_case)] on by default
src/main.rs:6     let fullLine = homeTeam.to_string() + result + awayTeam;

Pauls-MacBook-Pro:addstring-2 PFJ$ cargo build; cargo run
     Running `target/debug/addstring-2`
Liverpool beat Manchester United
```

What's with the warnings?

The recommended format that Rust uses is snake case (rather than CamelCase). The warnings can be removed if we change the variable name from homeTeam to home_team. It's not fatal, or likely to cause the program to go on a homicidal rampage; it's more of a style issue.

Using the format! macro

The format! macro works in a way similar to string formatters in other languages:

```
fn main() {
    let home_team = "Liverpool";
    let result = " beat ";
    let away_team = "Manchester United";
    let full_line = format!("{}{}{}", home_team, result, away_team);
    println!("{}", full_line);
}
```

The {} in the format strings mark spots for the following parameters. The spots are filled in order, so full_line will be a concatenation of home_team, result, and away_team.

When the preceding code snippet is compiled and executed, you will see the following:

```
Pauls-MacBook-Pro:formataddstring PFJ$ cargo build; cargo run
   Compiling formataddstring v0.1.0 (file:///Users/PFJ/Developer/rust/chapter1/formataddstri
ng)
     Running `target/debug/formataddstring`
Liverpool beat Manchester United
```

Building a string

We've seen that we can create a String from a string slice (using to_owned() or the format! macro), or we can create it using String::new().

There are two further ways to help build the string: push adds a single character to the string, and push_str adds an str to the string.

The following shows this in action:

```
fn main() {
    let home_team = "Liverpool";
    let result = " beat ";
    let away_team = "Manchester United";
```

```
let home_score = '3'; // single character
let away_score = "-0";

let mut full_line = format!("{}{}{} ", home_team, result, away_team);
// add the character to the end of the String
full_line.push(home_score);
// add the away score to the end of the String
full_line.push_str(away_score);
println!("{}", full_line);
}
```

When this last code snippet is compiled and executed, you will see this:

```
Pauls-MacBook-Pro:push-pushstr PFJ$ cargo build; cargo run
  Compiling push-pushstr v0.1.0 (file:///Users/PFJ/Developer/rust/chapter1/push-pushstr)
src/main.rs:8:9: 8:22        value assigned to `full_line` is never read, #[warn(unused_as
signments)] on by default
src/main.rs:8     let mut full_line = String::new();

  Running `target/debug/push-pushstr`
Liverpool beat Manchester United 3-0
```

Code review

The preceding code is somewhat different from the code in previous examples where we have simply used `to_owned()` to convert the slice to a string. We now have to create a mutable string and assign to that rather than just add to the end of `full_line` as we did previously.

The reason is that the slice being converted to string is not mutable; therefore, the type created will also be non-mutable. Since you cannot add to a non-mutable variable, we could not use the `push` and `push_str` methods.

Casting

Rust allows for variables to be cast differently. This is achieved using the `as` keyword. This works in the same way as it does in C#:

```
let my_score = 10i32;
let mut final_score : u32 = 100;
let final_score = my_score as u32;
```

We can also cast to a different type (for example, `float` to `int`):

```
let pi = 3.14;
let new_pi = pi as i32; // new_pi = 3
```

However, the effects of precision-losing casts like this one may not be desirable. For instance, if you cast a float that's over the bit size of `i8` to `i8`, the number gets truncated to `0`:

```
let n = 240.51;
let n_as_int = n as i8; // n_as_int = 0
```

An error will occur if the types you are attempting to cast to are not compatible; for example:

```
let my_home = "Newton-le-Willows";
let my_number = my_home as u32; // cannot convert &str to u32
```

Rust does not do implicit casting between primitive types, even when it would be safe. That is, if a function expects an `i8` as a parameter, you must cast an `i16` value to `i8` before passing it. The reason for this is to achieve the maximum type checking and, therefore, reduce the number of potential (and more problematic) hidden bugs.

String methods

Strings are important in any language. Without them, it becomes difficult to communicate with users, and if data is coming from a web service (in the form of XML, plain text, or JSON), this data will need to be manipulated. Rust provides the developer with a number of methods in the standard library to deal with strings. Here's a table of some useful methods (don't worry about the types yet):

Method	What it does	Usage (or example project)
`from(&str) -> String`	This method creates a new String from a string slice.	`let s = String::from("Richmond");`

`from_utf8( Vec < u8 > )` `-> Result<String,` `FromUtf8Error>`	This method creates a new string buffer from a valid vector of UTF-8 characters. It will fail if the vector contains non-UTF8 data.	`let s =` `String::from_utf8(vec!(33,` `34)).expect("UTF8 decoding` `failed);`
`with_capacity(usize) ->` `String`	This method preallocates a String with a number of bytes.	`let s =` `String::with_capacity(10);`
`as_bytes -> &[u8]`	This method outputs a String as a byte slice.	`let s = "A String".to_owned();` `let slice = s.as_bytes();`
`insert(usize, char)`	This method inserts `char` at position `index`.	`let mut s = "A` `String".to_owned();` `s.insert(2, 'S');` `// s = "A SString"`
`len -> usize`	This method returns the length of the String in bytes. It may therefore be larger than the number of characters in the String.	`let s = "A String äö";` `// s.len() => 13`
`is_empty -> bool`	This method returns `true` if the String is empty.	`let s1 = "".to_owned();` `let s2 = "A` `String".to_owned();` `// s1.is_empty() => true` `// s2.is_empty() => false`
`is_char_boundary(usize)` `-> bool`	This method returns `true` if a character at `index` falls on a Unicode boundary.	`let s1 = "Hellö World";` `// s1.is_char_boundary(5) =>` `false` `// s1.is_char_boundary(6) =>` `true`

Generics and arrays

For those coming from a C# or C++ background, you will no doubt be used to generic types (often referred to as having a type `T`); you will be used to seeing things like this:

```
T a = new T();
```

Generics allow defining methods for several types. In its most general form, `T` means "any type." The following function, for instance, takes two arguments that can be any type `T`:

```
fn generic_function<T>(a: T, b: T)
```

`T`, as has been established, can be of any type. This means that we cannot do much with them, since only a few methods are implemented for "any type." For instance, if we would like to add these variables together, we would need to restrict the generic types somewhat. We would essentially need to tell Rust that "T may be of any type, as long as it implements addition." More about this later.

Arrays

Arrays are simple to construct. For example:

```
let my_array = ["Merseybus", "Amberline", "Crosville", "Liverbus",
"Liverline", "Fareway"];
```

Arrays must comply with a number of rules, which are as follows:

- The array has a fixed size. It can never grow as it is stored as a continuous memory block.
- The contents of the array can only ever be of one type.

As with any type of variable, by default arrays are non-mutable. Even if the array is mutable, the overall size cannot be changed. For example, if an array has five elements, it cannot be changed to six.

We can also create an array with a type, as follows:

```
let mut my_array_two: [i32; 4] = [1, 11, 111, 1111];
let mut empty_array: [&str; 0] = [];
```

It is also possible to create an array a number of times with the same value, as follows:

```
let number = [111; 5];
```

This will create an array called `number` with 5 elements, all initialized to a value of `111`.

Array performance

While arrays are useful, they do have a performance hit; as with most operations on an array, the Rust runtime will perform bound checks to ensure the program does not access the array out of bounds. This prevents classic array overflow attacks and bugs.

Vectors

While arrays are simple to use, they have a single big disadvantage: they cannot be resized. The vector (`Vec`) acts in a way similar to a `List` in C#. It is also a generic type, as `Vec` itself is actually `Vec<T>`.

The `Vec` type is found in the standard library (`std::vec`).

To create a vector, we use something akin to either of the following:

```
let mut my_vector: Vec<f32> = Vec::new(); // explicit definition
```

Or this:

```
let mut my_alt_vector = vec![4f32, 3.14, 6.28, 13.54, 27.08];
```

The `f32` within the `Vec` macro tells the compiler that the type for the vector is `f32`. The `f32` can be omitted, as the compiler can determine the type for the vector.

Creating a vector with an initial size

As with a String, it is possible to create a vector with an initial allocation of memory, as follows:

```
let mut my_ids: Vec<i64> = Vec::with_capacity(30);
```

Creating a vector via an iterator

Another way to create a vector is via an iterator. This is achieved via the `collect()` method:

```
let my_vec: Vec<u64> = (0..10).collect();
```

 The format for the iterator is very convenient. Instead of the likes of `let foo = {0,1,2,3};`, this is shortened to use `..`, which means all numbers between *a* and *b* (*b* being excluded - so `0 .. 10` creates a vector containing 0,1,2,3,4,5,6,7,8,9). This can be seen in the source example supplied with this book.

Adding and removing from the vector

In a similar fashion to string, it is possible to add and remove from the vector list using the `push` and `pull` methods. These add or remove from the top of the vector stack. Consider the following example:

```
fn main() {
    let mut my_vec : Vec<i32> = (0..10).collect();
    println!("{:?}", my_vec);
    my_vec.push(13);
    my_vec.push(21);
    println!("{:?}", my_vec);
    let mut twenty_one = my_vec.pop(); // removes the last value
    println!("twenty_one= {:?}", twenty_one);
    println!("{:?}", my_vec);
}
```

We create the vector list with values from 0 going up to 10 (so the last value is 9).

The line `println!("{:?}", my_vec);` outputs the entire contents of `my_vec`. `{:?}` is required here due to the type `Vec<i32>` not implementing certain formatting functionalities.

We then push onto the top of the vector list 13 then 21, display the output on the screen, and then remove the top-most value on the vector list, and output it again.

Manipulating an array or vector via slices

Both arrays and vectors can be accessed using a value (such as `my_vec[4]`). However, if you want to manipulate a section of the array, then you would take a slice from the array. A slice is like a window to a part of the original thing.

To create a slice, use this:

```
let my_slice = &my_vec[1..5];
```

A slice also has no predefined size: it can be 2 bytes, or it can be 202 bytes. Due to this, the size of the slice is not known at compile time. This is important to know, because it prevents certain methods from working.

Passing values around

Up to this point, we have kept everything within a single method. For small demonstrations (or for method testing), this is fine. However, for larger applications, passing values between methods is essential.

Rust has two main ways to pass information to other methods: by reference or by value. Passing by reference usually implies borrowing, which means that ownership is only temporarily given and can be used again after the function call. Passing by value implies either a permanent ownership change, which means that the caller of a function can no longer access the value, or it might imply copying the data.

Passing by value

The following code shows how to pass a number between two functions, and to receive a result:

```
fn main()
{
    let add = add_values(3, 5);
    println!("{:?}", add);
}

fn add_values(a: i32, b: i32) -> i32
{
    a + b
}
```

Let's have a look at the receiving function's definition line:

```
fn add_values(a: i32, b: i32) -> i32
```

As with any programming language, we have to give the function a name, and then a parameter list. The parameter names are followed by a colon and the type of the parameter.

Our function returns a value (this is signified by the -> symbol) of a particular type (in this case, i32). The last evaluated thing in the function will be returned from the function, provided that you don't accidentally put a semi-colon there. An implicit return statement also exists, but it's not required and it's usually better style to omit it if possible.

When built and run, you will see the following:

```
Pauls-MacBook-Pro:pass_by_value PFJ$ cargo build; cargo run
   Compiling pass_by_value v0.1.0 (file:///Users/PFJ/Documents/Rust/Chapter%201%
20-%20Variables/Code/pass_by_value)
     Running `target/debug/pass_by_value`
8
```

Passing by reference

A variable passed by a reference looks like this:

```
fn my_function(a: &i32, b: &i32) -> i32
```

We take two variables as references, and return a value.

To obtain a value from a reference, the first thing to do is dereference it. This is done with the asterisk (*) operator:

```
let ref_num = &2;
let deref_num = *ref_num;
// deref_num = 2
```

The reference type

A reference is written in one of three ways: &, ref, or ref mut:

```
let mut var = 4;
let ref_to_var = &var;
let ref second_ref = var;
let ref mut third_ref = var;
```

The references are all equivalent here. Note, however, that the preceding code doesn't work as it is due to mutable reference rules. Rust allows several immutable reference to a thing, but if a mutable reference is taken, no other references may exist at the time. Therefore, the last line would not work, since there are already two active references to var.

A practical example

In the example code, `matrix`, we can see how to use a 2D array and how to pass by a reference, with the receiving function calculating the result of a matrix multiplication. Let's examine the code:

```
fn main()
{
    // first create a couple of arrays - these will be used
    // for the vectors
    let line1: [i32; 4] = [4, 2, 3, 3];
    let line2: [i32; 4] = [3, 4, 5, 7];
    let line3: [i32; 4] = [2, 9, 6, 2];
    let line4: [i32; 4] = [5, 7, 2, 4];

    // create two holding arrays and assign
    // we are creating an array of references
    let array_one = [&line1, &line3, &line4, &line2];
    let array_two = [&line2, &line1, &line3, &line4];

    // let's do the multiply
    // we are passing in a ref array containing ref arrays
    let result = matrix_multiply(&array_one, &array_two);
    println!("{:?}", result);
}

fn matrix_multiply(vec1: &[&[i32;4];4], vec2: &[&[i32;4];4]) -> [[i32;
4];4]
{
    // we need to create the arrays to put the results into
    let mut result = [[0i32; 4]; 4];

    // loop through the two vectors
    for vone in 0..4
    {
        for vtwo in 0..4
        {
            let mut sum = 0;
            for k in 0..4
            {
                sum += vec1[vone][k] * vec2[k][vtwo];
```

```
        }
        result[vone][vtwo] = sum;
      }
    }
    result
}
```

When compiled, you will get the following output:

```
Pauls-MacBook-Pro:matrix PFJ$ cargo build; cargo run
   Compiling matrix v0.1.0 (file:///Users/PFJ/Documents/Rust/Chapter%201%20-%20V
ariables/Code/matrix)
     Running `target/debug/matrix`
[[41, 68, 50, 52], [64, 94, 77, 61], [67, 80, 66, 76], [70, 114, 71, 71]]
```

What we need to really consider here is the definition line for the `matrix_multiply` function:

```
fn matrix_multiply(vec1: &[&[i32;4];4], vec2: &[&[i32;4];4]) -> [[i32;
4];4]
```

If you recall how we told a function the name of the variable and the type earlier, we said it was `variable_name: variable_type`. The preceding line may look very much different, but it really isn't:

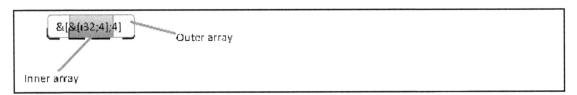

We are passing in a reference to a holding array, which holds references to other arrays. The array is defined using `[i32; 4]`; therefore, the reference is `&[i32; 4]`. This is the inner array. The outer array `[i32; 4]` is also a reference (`&[i32; 4]`), which has a size of 4. Therefore, when we put these together, we have the following:

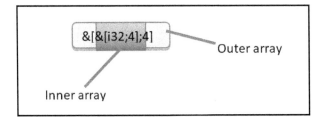

The preceding example shows how to pass by a reference quite nicely, though in reality, it is most likely that the compiler will optimize this out to something faster for such a small data sample. It does show, however, how it's done.

The golden rule is that what you send over to the function has to marry up with what the function is expecting.

Summary

We have covered a great deal in this chapter, and I really encourage you to play around creating functions and passing values around.

If you don't want to continually create new projects every time you create a new application, you can create and test your code on the Rust Playground website (https://play.rust-lang.org). Here you can enter your code, hit **Run**, and see instantly if what you have written works.

In the next chapter, we will be covering getting information in and out, and validating your entries.

3
Input and Output

Up to this point, we've only seen data coming from our examples, and then only using the `println!` macro function. While the `println!` macro is very useful, we really need to look at output. We also need to know how to get data in, and once the data is in, we have to check that the type entered is the type required.

In this chapter, we will be covering the following topics:

- Examining ways of outputting data
- Examining how to get data into an application
- Starting your program with command-line arguments
- Discussing how a method in Rust is different from a method in other languages
- A brief introduction to the standard library

Functions and methods in Rust

When we look at C++ or C#, a method is a programming unit within a class that does a specific task. A method in Rust is a function attached to compound data structures, or structs. These methods have access to the data of the object using the self parameter. They are defined in an `impl` block, as shown in the following example (a fuller example is given in the source examples):

```
struct Point {
    x: f64,
    y: f64
}

impl Point {
    fn origin() -> Point {
```

```
        Point {x: 0.0, y: 0.0 }
    }

    fn new(my_x: f64, my_y: f64) -> Point {
        Point { x: my_x, y: my_y }
    }
}
```

Here, we defined a struct, `Point`, for points in 2D space. Then, we defined two constructor methods for that struct: origin for making a new point in location 0,0 and another for making a new arbitrary point.

The difference between println! and println

Up to this point, we've used `println!` for outputting text. This is fine, but consider what `println!` does. Whenever you see a ! mark, it symbolizes a macro. Macros are used when some part of the function needs to be executed at compile time, rather than at runtime.

Consider the following:

```
println!("{}", a);
Console.WriteLine("{0}", a);
```

In C#, the preceding snippet will output a line with the value of a on the line. In this case, a can be of any type that supports conversion to a formatted output. The same applies to Rust. A line is output with the value of a.

The `println!` macro is actually implemented in the Rust standard library.

Introduction to the standard library

To be able to understand where `println!` comes from, we need to take a brief look at the Rust Standard Library. If you're familiar with C, C++, or C# (or any of the other languages commonly used), you'll have used something like this:

```
#include <stdio.h>
#include <stdlib>
using System.Collections.Generic;
```

These are standard libraries that the compiler comes with, and which the developer can optionally include. They contain many useful procedures, functions, and methods, all designed to make development simpler so that you don't need to keep reinventing the wheel when you need to do a common task.

A similar system exists in Rust in the form of crates. The std crate contains the Rust Standard Library, and it is by default included in every other crate. This means that you can use functionality from there without extra steps.

The crates are further separated into module hierarchies, with a double colon : : being a separator for the paths. So, for example, `std::fmt` is the `fmt` module inside the `std` module. It contains string formatting and printing functionality. For instance, the `println!` macro that we have used already is there.

So why don't we have to write `std::fmt::println!` every time we use the `println!` macro? Because `println!` is one of the many standard macros which are imported to every namespace automatically.

You can also import things to the current namespace yourself, to save yourself some keystrokes. This is done by the use keyword. Here's an example that uses the `HashMap` collection type from the standard library, without using the use keyword:

```
let mut my_hashmap: std::collections::HashMap<String, u8> =
    std::collections::HashMap::new();
my_hashmap.insert("one".to_owned(), 1);
```

Spelling out the full namespace explicitly every time is possible, but as you can see, the noise-to-signal ratio is a bit poorer. Importing the `HashMap` into the current namespace can help. This piece of code is equivalent to the previous:

```
use std::collections::HashMap;
let mut my_hashmap: HashMap<String, u8> = HashMap::new();
my_hashmap.insert("one".to_owned(), 1);
```

Rust's library system is a bit different from other languages, and may therefore be a bit of a stumbling block for newcomers. I found it a useful tidbit to realize that use clauses are not required to make code visible and callable: they just import a namespace into the current namespace.

The libraries

The `std` libraries define the primitives we have already encountered (`array`, different sized floats and integers, `String`, and so on), but also contain a number of other modules. They also define the commonly used macros (such as `write!` and `println!`).

For the purposes of this chapter, we will cover only `std::io`, `std::fs`, and `std::fmt`. These deal with input/output, the filesystem, and formatting. The `io` and `fs` modules will be dealt with later in this chapter.

Controlling the output formatting

The `std::fmt` module provides the developer with a range of utilities for formatting and printing strings. Let's start with the `format!` macro. This macro returns a string.

We have seen that if we use `println!(Hello {}, myString)`, the code will print the contents of `myString` after the `Hello`. The `format!` macro works pretty much the same, just that it returns the formatted string instead of outputting it. In fact, `println!` essentially uses `format!` itself under the hood.

Positioning the output

One of the more useful extensions in C# is `string.Format(...);`. This allows for a string to be constructed based on parameters at particular positions. For example, the following statement constructs a string where the parameter at a position after the string literal is inserted into the string (here, the letter `B` is inserted twice in the middle of the string and then at the end):

```
var myString = string.Format("Hello {0}, I am a {1}{1}{2} computer model
{1}", name, "B", "C");
```

Rust also supports this form, but with the difference that the positioning may be omitted.

Consider the following examples:

```
format!("{} {}", 2, 10); // output 2 10
format!("{1} {} {0} {}", "B", "A");
```

The first example is what we've seen before. The format string gets filled with the parameters on the right, in order.

In the second example, it would seem that we're asking for four parameters, but have only supplied two. The way this works is that the positional arguments are ignored when filling in the non-positional arguments. Indexing, as is usual in programming, starts at zero. This is how the arguments are processed:

- {1} inserts the second parameter A
- {} inserts the first parameter B
- {0} inserts the first parameter B
- {} inserts the second parameter A

Therefore, the output is going to be **A B B A**.

The following are the two important rules governing the positional parameters:

1. All of the arguments within the quotes must be used. Failure to do so will result in a compiler error.
2. You can refer to the same argument as many times as you like within the format string.

Named parameters

As shown in the formatting table, it is possible to use a named parameter. The operation of these is similar to a positional parameter; the difference, though, is that a named parameter is used. This is very useful in ensuring that the value output in the string is the correct parameter.

It is perfectly acceptable to use an empty parameter within a formatted string when using a named parameter, for example:

```
format!("{b} {a} {} {t}", b = "B", a = 'a', t = 33);
```

The rules for handling non-positional parameters alongside named parameters are similar to the rules for positional parameters: the named parameters are ignored when figuring out the positions. This will, therefore, give the output **B a B 33**.

Specifying the argument types

As with much of the string handling in the C family of languages, it is possible to create a string based on a format string (for example, {0:##.###} would give a formatted output of the form **xy.abc**).

Similar things can be done in Rust, as follows:

```
let my_number = format!("{:.3}", 3.1415927);
```

In the format string, the colon says we're requesting formatting for the value. Dot and 3 says that we want the number formatted to three decimal points. The formatter rounds the value for us, so the output will be **3.142.**

Formatting traits

Formatting traits determine how the output of the format will be produced. They are all used in the same way: {:trait_name}.

The following are the current traits available:

Format string	Trait	Meaning	Example
{}	Display	A human-readable representation. Not all things implement Display.	123 => "123"
{:?}	Debug	An internal representation. Almost everything implements Debug.	b"123" => [49, 50, 51]
{:b}	Binary	Converts a number into binary	123 => "1111011"
{:x}	LowerHex	Hex in lowercase	123 => 7b
{:X}	UpperHex	Hex in uppercase	123 => 7B
{:e}	LowerExp	Number with exponential, lowercase	123.0 => 1.23e2
{:E}	UpperExp	Number with exponential, uppercase	123.0 => 1.23E2
{:p}	Pointer	Pointer location	&123 => 0x55b3fbe72980 (may point to a different address on every run)

Similarly, the output can be formatted with formatting parameters.

Formatting parameters

There are essentially four formatting parameters available. They are listed in the following table:

Parameter	Use
`Fill/Alignment`	Used in conjunction with the `Width` parameter. Essentially, this will add extra characters if the output is smaller than the width.
`Sign/#/0`	Flags for the formatter being used: • `Sign` indicates that the sign should always be outputted (numeric values only). If the value is positive, the + sign will never show; similarly, a – will only show for a `Signed` value. • # indicates that an alternate form of printing will be used. Normally, if `{:x}` is used, the lowercase hex format is used. By using `#x`, the argument is preceded with `0x`. • `0` is used to pad a result with the `0` character. It is sign-aware.
`Width`	Specifies how the output should be represented. For example, if you have a float calculation that has to be outputted to four decimal places, and the result only comes to two decimal places, the width formatter (in conjunction with the fill formatting parameter) will create the required filled output.
`Precision`	For anything non-numeric, the precision is the maximum width. For example, if you have a maximum width of five and a string containing eight characters, it will be truncated after five characters. It is ignored for integers. For floating point types, it indicates the number of decimal points after the point: • Integer `.N::` In this case, N is the precision. • Integer followed by a `$` (`.N$:`): This uses the format argument N as the precision. The argument must be a `usize`. • `.*::` This means that the contents of the `{}` is associated with two format inputs. The first holds the `usize` precision, the second holds the value to be printed.

Examples of all of these formatters are in the source code examples for this chapter.

Getting information in

Up to this point, we have concentrated on getting information out from a Rust program rather than entering information.

Input is done via the `std::io` module, getting a reader using the `io::stdin()` function, and then calling `read_line` on that reader. We put the inputted data into a dynamically growing `String`, which needs to be mutable.

A simple example for inputting would look like this:

```
// 03/readline/src/main.rs
use std::io;
fn main() {
    let reader: io::Stdin = io::stdin();
    let mut input_text: String = String::new();

    reader.read_line(&mut input_text).expect("Reading failed");
    println!("Read {}", input_text);
}
```

We can see Rust's error handling in action in the previous code. The `read_line` method returns a result type, which means that the operation could have failed. The result type encapsulates two generic types inside itself, which in the case of `read_line` are `usize` (for reporting how many bytes were read in) and `io::Error` (for reporting any errors during input). The actual read String is placed in the first argument of the function, in this case `input_text`.

On that result type, our example calls the `expect` method. It expects that everything went fine, and returns the first value (the `usize` in this case). If there were errors, the `expect` method prints reading failed to the standard output and exits the program.

This is not the only way to handle result types, but it's a common one in cases where we expect things to usually work out fine.

Another way to handle the error is to explicitly call the `is_err` method on the result. It returns a boolean, like this:

```
let result: Result<usize, io::Error> = reader.read_line(&mut
input_text);
    if result.is_err() {
        println!("failed to read from stdin");
        return;
    }
```

If we wish to further parse the entry into another type, we can use the `parse` method.

For instance, say we'd like to get an `i32` from the input. The `read_line` method includes a carriage return in the input data, so we need to get rid of that using the `trim` method before parsing:

```
let trimmed = input_text.trim();
let option: Option<i32> = trimmed.parse::<i32>().ok();
```

For the sake of this example, this final line converts the result type into an `Option` using the `ok` method. Option is a simplified version of result. This is a useful library and it can have one of two results: `Some` or `None`.

Here, if the entry result is `None`, the value is not an integer, whereas `Some` would be an integer:

```
match option {
        Some(i) => println!("your integer input: {}", i),
        None => println!("this was not an integer: {}", trimmed)
    };
```

Command-line arguments

When a program is started, it can be started with or without arguments. These arguments are normally fed in as parameters when the program is called. A simple example of this is starting the manual application (found on many BSD and Linux machines):

```
man ffmpeg
```

In the preceding statement, man is the name of the program or script to be called with the argument ffmpeg. Similarly, take a look at the following example for Windows users:

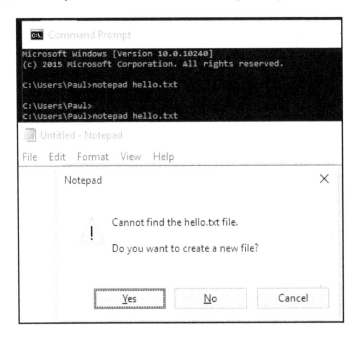

Notepad is the program name with the first argument being the file to read in (in this example, the file doesn't exist, so the UI asks if you wish to create it).

It is not uncommon for one program to load another program to perform a task.

In C, the parameter list for main is given as follows:

```
int main(int argc, char *argv[])
```

argc is the maximum number of arguments with argv holding the arguments. Here, the program name is argv[0], so all additional arguments start at 1.

Rust's main takes no arguments like this. Command-line parameters are available through the standard library std::env::args (environment arguments). For simplicity, it is convenient to store the arguments in Vec<String>, because env::args returns an iterator that yields a String.

No parameters are passed into `main` directly:

```
// 03/args/src/main.rs
use std::env;
fn main() {
    let args: Vec<String> = env::args().collect();
    println!("There was {:?} arguments passed in. They were {:?}.",
args.len() - 1, &args[1..]);
}
```

The `collect` method converts the iterator into a vector, making it possible to access it by indexing. Without it, we would have to go through the arguments one by one.

Handling files

The final part of our tour of getting information in and out of a program is using files. As far as Rust is concerned, a file is just another stream, with the exception that this stream goes elsewhere.

It is important when using anything to do with files that the `try!` macro is used to trap all errors.

Reading from a file

Here, we are going to use `std::io`, `std::io::prelude::*` and `std::fs::File`. `std::io` is the standard input/output library, the `*` after prelude means to use anything in the prelude library, and `std::fs` is the filesystem library.

> Filesystem calls are very platform-specific; Windows users use the likes of `C://Users/Paul/Documents/My Documents` for the user's home directory, whereas Linux and macOS machines would use `~/` for the user's home directory. If a path is not given for a file, the program will assume the file is in the same directory in which the binary resides.

Loading a file

To open a file, we use `File::open(filename)`. We can catch exceptions using the `try!` macro or `match`, as follows:

```
let file = try!(File::open("my_file.txt"))
```

Or the following can be used:

```
let file = match File::open("my_file.txt") {
    Ok(file) => file,
    Err(..) => panic!("boom"),
}
```

If the file is available to open, `File::open` will grant read permissions to the file. To load the file, we create a `BufReader` based on the file:

```
let mut reader = BufReader::new(&file);
let buffer_string = &mut String::new();
reader.read_line(buffer_string);
println!("Line read in: {}", buffer_string);
```

Once the file has been read, the stream can be explicitly closed with `reader.close()`. However, Rust's resource management system guarantees that the file will be closed when its binding goes out of scope, so this is not mandatory.

Writing a file

Writing to a file is a two-step process: opening the file (possibly creating it if it didn't exist before) and then the writing of the file. This is very similar to how writing to a file in the C family of languages is carried out.

You can create a file for writing in a single call to `std::fs::File::create`. The `open` method in the same namespace opens a file for reading. If you need more fine-tuned permissions, `std::fs::OpenOptions::new` creates an object through which you can tweak the parameters and then open the file.

As with any file operation, anything could fail, so the result should always be checked:

```
let file: Result<File,Error> = options.open(path);
```

As mentioned before, Rust uses a generic type, `Result<T,U>`, quite frequently as an error-trapping mechanism. It encapsulates two values: the left-hand side value is used when the operation succeeds, and the right-hand side value is used when it does not succeed.

Once we have completed the file creation, we can move on to writing to the file.

First, we check the results of the `Result` comparison. If an error hasn't been thrown there was no error, and we can then create a `BufWriter`:

```
let mut writer = BufWriter::new(&file);
writer.write_all(b"hello text file\n");
```

We don't need to flush the buffer, as `write_all` will do that for us (it calls `flush()` once completed). If you don't use `write_all`, then you need to call `flush()` to ensure the buffer is cleared.

The use of expect

Rust contains a very useful function called `expect`. This method is used with any form of call that has an `Option` or a `Result` type (for example, `Result` in the file-writing example has the options of `File` or `Error`). It works by moving the value out of the option and returning it. If the `option/result` type contains an error, the `expect` call stops your program and prints out the error message.

For example, the following statement will return either `File` or `Error` into `file`:

```
let file: Result<File, Error> = options.open("my_file.txt").expect("Opening
the file failed");
```

A shorter form is available in the `unwrap` method. This is the same as the `expect` method, but it doesn't print out anything in case of a failure. In general, `Some(a).unwrap()` will return `a`.

`Expect` is usually favored instead of `unwrap`, since the full error message makes it easier to find where the error came from.

XML and Rust

As Rust is well suited to running on servers, it seems appropriate that we consider XML, and how it is handled within Rust.

Thankfully, Rust comes with a crate called `Xml`, which works in a way similar to how standard streams are read and written.

Reading a file

As with a standard file, we first have to open the file and create a reader:

```
let file = File::open("my_xmlfile.xml").unwrap();
let reader =BufferedReader::new(file);
```

Next, we start the reading. Unlike a normal reader, we use `EventReader`. This provides a number of events (such as `StartElement`, `EndElement`, and `Error`), which are required for reading in from the differing nodes:

```
let mut xml_parser = EventReader::new(reader);
```

Next, we iterate through the file, as follows:

```
for e in xml_parser.events() {
    match e {
        StartElement { name, .. } => {
            println!("{}", name);
        }
        EndElement {name} => {
            println!("{}", name);
        }
        Error(e) => {
            println!("Error in file: {}", e);
        }
        _ => {}
    }
}
```

In the preceding snippet, `_ => {}` essentially means that you don't care what is left, do something with it (in this case, the something is nothing). You will see the symbol _ quite a bit in Rust. Commonly, it is used in loops where the variable being acted on is never used, for example:

```
for _ in something() {...}
```

We aren't going to use the iterator; we just need something to enable the iteration to go to the next value.

Writing a file

Writing an XML file is far more complex than reading. Here, we have to explicitly use `XmlEvent` and `EventWriter`. We also use `EmitterConfig`, which does as the name suggests, that is, creates a configuration and then uses it. `EventWriter`, `EmitterConfig`, and `XmlEvent` are all part of `xml::writer`.

Let us first consider the main function. First, create the file and two references, one to `stdin` and one to `stdout`, as follows:

```
let mut file = File::create("myxml_file.xml).unwrap();
let mut output = io::stdout();
let mut input = io::stdin();
```

Next, we create the writer via `EmitterConfig`:

```
let mut writer =
EmitterConfig::new().preform_indent(true).create_writer(&mut file);
```

We now have the writer set up. `perform_indent` tells the writer to indent each node when true.

Finally, we create a loop and write the XML. You will notice a call to `handle_event`; we will deal with this shortly:

```
loop {
    print!("> ");
    output.flush().unwrap();
    let mut line = String::new();
    match input.readline(&mut line) {
        Ok(0) => break,
        Ok(_) => match handle_event(&mut writer, line) {
            Ok(_) => {}
            Err(e) => panic!("XML write error: {}", e)
        }
        Err(e) => panic!("Input error: {}", e);
    }
}
```

The definition of the function `handle_event` is a bit more advanced than we have seen until now:

```
fn handle_event<W: Write>(w: &mut EventWriter<W>, line: String) ->
Result<()> {
```

In C#, the preceding definition would be something similar, and would be written as follows:

```
Result handle_result<T>(EventWriter<T> w, string line) where T:Write
```

We pass a type (be it a `class`, `string`, `i32`, or anything else for that matter) to the function to use as a parameter. In this case, we are using `std::io::Write` for the `EventWriter` to use.

The function itself has nothing special. We start by trimming the string to remove any whitespace or returns:

```
let line = line.trim();
```

We now use `XmlEvent` to generate the code:

```
let event: XmlEvent = if line.starts_with("+") && line.len() > 1 {
    XmlEvent::start_element(&line[1..]).into()
} else if line.starts_with("-") {
    XmlEvent::end_element().into()
} else {
    XmlEvent::characters(&line).into()
    };
    w.write(&line).into();
}
```

`into()` converts the pointer to the structure (known as `self`). In this case, it takes (say) `XmlEvent::characters(&line)`, and sends it back into the line.

Summary

We have covered quite a lot of material in this chapter, and you should feel more at home with handling strings, XML, and files, which can be used to add further functionality to your code. Please feel free to examine the examples supplied for this chapter.

In the next chapter, we will have a look at loops, recursion, and branching.

4
Conditions, Recursion, and Loops

Loops and conditions within any programming language are a fundamental aspect of operation. You may be looping around a list attempting to find when something matches, and when a match occurs, branching out to perform some other task; or, you may just want to check a value to see whether it meets a condition. In any case, Rust allows you to do this.

In this chapter, we will cover the following topics:

- Types of loop available
- Different types of branching within loops
- Recursive methods
- When the semicolon (;) can be omitted and what it means

Loops

Rust has essentially three types of loops:

- `loop` is the simplest one—it just goes through a block of code again and again until one of the loop-breaking keywords is used
- `while` is like loop, but with a condition—the block of code is looped again and again as long as the condition is true
- `for` is different from the above two—it is for iterating through sequences

The for loop

The `for` loops are slightly different from the same construct in C-like languages. In C, the `for` loops consist of three things: an initialization, a stopping condition, and a stepping instruction. Rust `for` loops are a bit higher-level though: they are for iterating through sequences.

Let's take a simple example to start with—a loop that goes from 0 to 10 and outputs the value:

```
for x in 0..10
{
    println!("{},", x);
}
```

We create a variable x that takes an element from the range (0..10), one by one, and does something with it. In Rust terminology, 0..10 is not only a variable but also an **iterator**, as it gives back a value from a series of elements.

This is obviously a very simple example. We can also define the iterator to work in the opposite direction. In C, you will expect something akin to `for (i = 10; i > 0; --i)`. In Rust, we use the `rev()` method to reverse the iterator, as follows:

```
for x in (0..10).rev()
{
    println!("{},", x);
}
```

It is worth noting that the range excludes the last number. So, for the previous example, the values outputted are 9 to 0; essentially, the program generates the output values from 0 to 10 and then outputs them in reverse.

The general syntax for the `for` loops is as follows:

```
for var in sequence
{
    // do something
}
```

The C# equivalent for the preceding code is as follows:

```
foreach(var t in conditionsequence)
    // do something
```

Using enumerate

A loop condition can also be more complex, using multiple conditions and variables. For example, the for loop can be tracked using enumerate. This will keep track of how many times the loop has executed, as shown here:

```
for(i, j) in (10..20).enumerate()
{
    println!("loop has executed {} times. j = {}", i, j);
}
```

The following is the output:

```
enumerate — -bash — 80×11
loop has executed 0 times. j = 10
loop has executed 1 times. j = 11
loop has executed 2 times. j = 12
loop has executed 3 times. j = 13
loop has executed 4 times. j = 14
loop has executed 5 times. j = 15
loop has executed 6 times. j = 16
loop has executed 7 times. j = 17
loop has executed 8 times. j = 18
loop has executed 9 times. j = 19
Pauls-MacBook-Pro:enumerate PFJ$
```

Say we have an array that we need to iterate over to obtain the values. Here, the enumerate method can be used to obtain the value of the array members. The value returned in the condition will be a reference, so a code such as the one shown in the following example will fail to execute (line is a & reference whereas an i32 is expected):

```
// 04/enumerate/src/main.rs
fn main()
{
    let my_array: [i32; 7] = [1i32,3,5,7,9,11,13];
    let mut value = 0i32;
    for(_, line) in my_array.iter().enumerate()
    {
        value += line;
    }
    println!("{}", value);
}
```

This can be simply converted back from the reference value, as follows:

```
for(_, line) in my_array.iter().enumerate()
    {
        value += *line;
    }
```

The `iter().enumerate()` method can equally be used with the `Vec` type (or any other type that implements the iterator trait), as shown in the following code:

```
// 04/arrayloop/src/main.rs
fn main()
{
    let my_array = vec![1i32,3,5,7,9,11,13];
    let mut value = 0i32;

    for(_,line) in my_array.iter().enumerate()
    {
        value += *line;
    }
    println!("{}", value);
}
```

In both cases, the value given at the end will be `49`, as shown in the following screenshot:

```
arrayloop — -bash — 80×20
Pauls-MacBook-Pro:arrayloop PFJ$ cargo run
    Compiling arrayloop v0.1.0 (file:///Users/PFJ/Dropbox/Rust/Chapter%204%20-%20
Recursion/Code/arrayloop)
    Running `target/debug/arrayloop`
49
```

The _ parameter

You may be wondering what the _ parameter is. In Rust, it is often not allowed to omit variable bindings even if we don't use them. We can use _ to signify that we know that this place needs a variable binding, but we are never going to use it.

The simple loop

A simple form of the loop is called `loop`:

```
loop
{
    println!("Hello");
}
```

The preceding code has no loop-ending keywords, such as break; it will output `Hello` until the application is terminated manually.

The while condition

The `while` condition extends the loop with a condition, as you will see in the following code snippet:

```
while (condition)
{
    // do something
}
```

Let's take a look at the following example:

```
fn main() {
    let mut done = 0u32;
    while done != 32
    {
        println!("done = {}", done);
        done += 1;
    }
}
```

The preceding code will output `done` = 0 to `done` = 31. The loop terminates when `done` equals 32.

Prematurely terminating a loop

Depending on the size of the data being iterated over within a loop, the loop can be costly on processor time. For example, say the server is receiving data from a data-logging application, such as measuring values from a gas chromatograph; over the entire scan, it may record roughly half a million data points with an associated time position.

For our purposes, we want to add all of the recorded values until the value is over 1.5 and once that is reached, we can stop the loop.

Sound easy? There is one thing not mentioned: there is no guarantee that the recorded value will ever reach over 1.5, so how can we terminate the loop if the value is reached?

We can do this in one of two ways. The first is to use a `while` loop and introduce a Boolean to act as the test condition. In the following example, `my_array` represents a very small subsection of the data sent to the server:

```
// 04/terminate-loop-1/src/main.rs
fn main()
{
    let my_array = vec![0.6f32, 0.4, 0.2, 0.8, 1.3, 1.1, 1.7, 1.9];
    let mut counter: usize = 0;
    let mut result = 0f32;
    let mut quit = false;

    while quit != true
    {
        if my_array[counter] > 1.5
        {
            quit = true;
        }
        else
        {
            result += my_array[counter];
            counter += 1;
        }
    }
     println!("{}", result);
}
```

The result here is 4.4. This code is perfectly acceptable, if slightly long-winded. Rust also allows the use of the `break` and `continue` keywords (if you're familiar with C, they work in the same way).

Our code using `break` will be as follows:

```
// 04/terminate-loop-2/src/main.rs
fn main()
{
    let my_array = vec![0.6f32, 0.4, 0.2, 0.8, 1.3, 1.1, 1.7, 1.9];
    let mut result = 0f32;

    for(_, value) in my_array.iter().enumerate()
    {
```

```
    if *value > 1.5
    {
        break;
    }
    else
    {
        result += *value;
    }
}
println!("{}", result);
}
```

Again, this will give an answer of 4.4, indicating that the two methods used are equivalent.

If we replace break with continue in the preceding code example, we will get the same result (4.4). The difference between break and continue is that continue jumps to the next value in the iteration rather than jumping out, so if we had the final value of my_array as 1.3, the output at the end should be 5.7.

 When using break and continue, always keep in mind this difference. While it may not crash the code, mistaking break and continue may lead to results that you may not expect or want.

Using loop labels

Rust allows us to label our loops. This can be very useful, for example with nested loops. These labels act as symbolic names for the loop and as we have a name for the loop, we can instruct the application to perform a task on that name.

Consider the following simple example:

```
// 04/looplabels/src/main.rs
fn main()
{
    'outer_loop: for x in 0..10
    {
        'inner_loop: for y in 0..10
        {
            if x % 2 == 0 { continue 'outer_loop; }
            if y % 2 == 0 { continue 'inner_loop; }
            println!("x: {}, y: {}", x, y);
        }
    }
}
```

What will this code do?

Here, x % 2 == 0 (or y % 2 == 0) means that if a variable divided by two returns no remainder, then the condition is met and it executes the code in the braces. When x % 2 == 0, or when the value of the loop is an even number, we will tell the application to skip to the next iteration of outer_loop, which is an odd number. However, we will also have an inner loop. Again, when y % 2 is an even value, we will tell the application to skip to the next iteration of inner_loop.

In this case, the application will output the following results:

```
looplabels — -bash — 80×28
Pauls-MacBook-Pro:looplabels PFJ$ cargo run
     Running `target/debug/looplabels`
x: 1, y: 1
x: 1, y: 3
x: 1, y: 5
x: 1, y: 7
x: 1, y: 9
x: 3, y: 1
x: 3, y: 3
x: 3, y: 5
x: 3, y: 7
x: 3, y: 9
x: 5, y: 1
x: 5, y: 3
x: 5, y: 5
x: 5, y: 7
x: 5, y: 9
x: 7, y: 1
x: 7, y: 3
x: 7, y: 5
x: 7, y: 7
x: 7, y: 9
x: 9, y: 1
x: 9, y: 3
x: 9, y: 5
x: 9, y: 7
x: 9, y: 9
Pauls-MacBook-Pro:looplabels PFJ$ 
```

While this example may seem very simple, it does allow for a great deal of speed when checking data. Let's go back to our previous example of data being sent to the web service. Recall that we have two values—the recorded data and some other value; for ease, it will be a data point. Each data point is recorded 0.2 seconds apart; therefore, every fifth data point is one second.

This time, we want all of the values where the data is greater than 1.5 and the associated time of that data point, but only on a time when it's dead on a second. As we want the code to be understandable and human-readable, we can use a loop label on each loop.

The following code is not quite correct. Can you spot why? The code compiles as follows:

```
// 04/looplabels-2/src/main.rs
fn main()
{
    let my_array = vec![0.6f32, 0.4, 0.2, 0.8, 1.3, 1.1, 1.7, 1.9, 1.3,
0.1, 1.6, 0.6, 0.9, 1.1, 1.31, 1.49, 1.5, 0.7];
    let my_time = vec![0.2f32, 0.4, 0.6, 0.8, 1.0, 1.2, 1.4, 1.6, 1.8, 2.0,
2.2, 2.4, 2.6, 2.8, 3.0, 3.2, 3.4, 3.6, 3.8];

    'time_loop: for(_, time_value) in my_time.iter().enumerate()
    {
        'data_loop: for(_, value) in my_array.iter().enumerate()
        {
            if *value < 1.5
            {
                continue 'data_loop;
            }
            if *time_value % 5f32 == 0f32
            {
                continue 'time_loop;
            }
            println!("Data point = {} at time {}s", *value, *time_value);
        }
    }
}
```

This example is a very good one to demonstrate the correct operator in use. The issue is the `if *time_value % 5f32 == 0f32` line. We are taking a float value and using the modulus of another float to see whether we end up with 0 as a float.

Comparing any value that is not a `string`, `int`, `long`, or `bool` type to another is never a good plan, especially if the value is returned by some form of calculation. We can also not simply use `continue` on the time loop, so how can we solve this problem?

If you recall, we're using _ instead of a named parameter for the enumeration of the loop. These values are always an integer; therefore, if we replace _ for a variable name, then we can use `% 5` to perform the calculation and the code becomes the following:

```
'time_loop: for(time_enum, time_value) in my_time.iter().enumerate()
    {
        'data_loop: for(_, value) in my_array.iter().enumerate()
        {
```

```
            if *value < 1.5
            {
                continue 'data_loop;
            }
            if time_enum % 5 == 0
            {
                continue 'time_loop;
            }
            println!("Data point = {} at time {}s", *value, *time_value);
        }
    }
```

The next problem is that the output isn't correct. The code gives the following:

```
Data point = 1.7 at time 0.4s
Data point = 1.9 at time 0.4s
Data point = 1.6 at time 0.4s
Data point = 1.5 at time 0.4s
Data point = 1.7 at time 0.6s
Data point = 1.9 at time 0.6s
Data point = 1.6 at time 0.6s
Data point = 1.5 at time 0.6s
```

The data point is correct, but the time is way out and continually repeats. We still need the continue statement for the data point step, but the time step is incorrect. There are a couple of solutions, but possibly the simplest will be to store the data and the time in a new vector and then display that data at the end.

The following code gets closer to what is required:

```
// 04/looplabels-3/src/main.rs
fn main()
{
    let my_array = vec![0.6f32, 0.4, 0.2, 0.8, 1.3, 1.1, 1.7, 1.9, 1.3,
0.1, 1.6, 0.6, 0.9, 1.1, 1.31, 1.49, 1.5, 0.7];
    let my_time = vec![0.2f32, 0.4, 0.6, 0.8, 1.0, 1.2, 1.4, 1.6, 1.8, 2.0,
2.2, 2.4, 2.6, 2.8, 3.0, 3.2, 3.4, 3.6, 3.8];
    let mut my_new_array = vec![];
    let mut my_new_time = vec![];

    'time_loop: for(t, _) in my_time.iter().enumerate()
    {
        'data_loop: for(v, value) in my_array.iter().enumerate()
        {
            if *value < 1.5
            {
                continue 'data_loop;
            }
```

```
            else
            {
                if t % 5 != 0
                {
                    my_new_array.push(*value);
                    my_new_time.push(my_time[v]);
                }
            }
            if v == my_array.len()
            {
                break;
            }
        }
    }
    for(m, my_data) in my_new_array.iter().enumerate()
    {
        println!("Data = {} at time {}", *my_data, my_new_time[m]);
    }
}
```

We will now get the following output:

```
Data = 1.7 at time 1.4
Data = 1.9 at time 1.6
Data = 1.6 at time 2.2
Data = 1.5 at time 3.4
Data = 1.7 at time 1.4
```

Yes, we now have the correct data, but the time starts again. We're close, but it's not right yet. We aren't continuing the `time_loop` loop and we will also need to introduce a `break` statement. To trigger the `break`, we will create a new variable called `done`. When v, the enumerator for `my_array`, reaches the length of the vector (this is the number of elements in the vector), we will change this from `false` to `true`. This is then tested outside of the `data_loop`. If `done == true`, break out of the loop.

The final version of the code is as follows:

```
// 04/dataloop/src/main.rs
fn main()
{
    let my_array = vec![0.6f32, 0.4, 0.2, 0.8, 1.3, 1.1, 1.7, 1.9, 1.3,
0.1, 1.6, 0.6, 0.9, 1.1, 1.31, 1.49, 1.5, 0.7];
    let my_time = vec![0.2f32, 0.4, 0.6, 0.8, 1.0, 1.2, 1.4, 1.6, 1.8, 2.0,
2.2, 2.4, 2.6, 2.8, 3.0, 3.2, 3.4, 3.6];
    let mut my_new_array = vec![];
    let mut my_new_time = vec![];
    let mut done = false;
```

```rust
'time_loop: for(t, _) in my_time.iter().enumerate()
{
    'data_loop: for(v, value) in my_array.iter().enumerate()
    {
        if v == my_array.len() - 1
        {
            done = true;
        }
        if *value < 1.5
        {
            continue 'data_loop;
        }
        else
        {
            if t % 5 != 0
            {
                my_new_array.push(*value);
                my_new_time.push(my_time[v]);
            }
            else
            {
                continue 'time_loop;
            }
        }
    }
    if done {break;}
}
for(m, my_data) in my_new_array.iter().enumerate()
{
    println!("Data = {} at time {}", *my_data, my_new_time[m]);
}
}
```

Our final output from the code is this:

```
Pauls-MacBook-Pro:dataloop PFJ$ cargo run
   Compiling dataloop v0.1.0 (file:///Users/PFJ/Dropbox/Rust/Chapter%204%20-%20R
ecursion/Code/dataloop)
     Running `target/debug/dataloop`
Data = 1.7 at time 1.4
Data = 1.9 at time 1.6
Data = 1.6 at time 2.2
Data = 1.5 at time 3.4
Pauls-MacBook-Pro:dataloop PFJ$ 
```

Recursive functions

The final form of loop to consider is known as a **recursive function**. This is a function that calls itself until a condition is met. In pseudocode, the function looks like this:

```
float my_function(i32:a: i32)
{
    // do something with a
    if (a != 32)
    {
        my_function(a);
    }
    else
    {
        return a;
    }
}
```

An actual implementation of a recursive function would look like this:

```
// 04/recurse-1/src/main.rs
fn recurse(n: i32)
{
    let v = match n % 2
    {
        0 => n / 2,
        _ => 3 * n + 1
    };
    println!("{}", v);
    if v != 1
    {
        recurse(v)
    }
}

fn main()
{
    recurse(25)
}
```

The idea of a recursive function is very simple, but we need to consider two parts of this code. The first is the `let` line in the `recurse` function and what it means:

```
let v = match n % 2
    {
        0 => n / 2,
        _ => 3 * n + 1
    };
```

Another way of writing this is as follows:

```
let mut v = 0i32;
if n % 2 == 0
{
    v = n / 2;
}
else
{
    v = 3 * n + 1;
}
```

The second part is that the semicolon is not being used everywhere. Consider the following example:

```
fn main()
{
    recurse(25)
}
```

What is the difference between having and not having a semicolon?

In Rust, almost everything is an expression. This means that almost everything returns a value. One exception is the variable binding statement `let`. In a `let` statement, and many others, the ending semicolon is a mandatory part of the syntax.

However, in expressions, the semicolon has a double role: it throws away a return value of the expression in addition to allowing further expressions. So if the expression is the last in a block, having a semicolon there means that the last value is thrown away, and not having a semicolon there means to return the last value.

An example should make it clear:

```
// 04/semicolon_block/src/main.rs
fn main()
{
    let x = 5u32;

    let y =
    {
        let x_squared = x * x;
        let x_cube = x_squared * x;
        x_cube + x_squared + x
    };
```

```
let z =
{
    2 * x;
};

println!("x is {:?}", x);
println!("y is {:?}", y);
println!("z is {:?}", z);
}
```

We have two different uses of the semicolon. Let's look at the `let y` line first:

```
let y =
    {
        let x_squared = x * x;
        let x_cube = x_squared * x;
        x_cube + x_squared + x // no semi-colon
    };
```

This code does the following:

- The code within the braces is processed
- The final line, without the semicolon, is assigned to `y`

Essentially, this is considered as an inline function that returns the line without the semicolon into the variable.

The second line to consider is for `z`:

```
let z =
{
    2 * x;
};
```

Again, the code within the braces is evaluated. In this case, the line ends with a semicolon, so the result is thrown away and the empty value `()` gets bound to `z`.

When it is executed, we will get the following results:

```
                     semicolon_block — -bash — 80×7
    Compiling semicolon_block v0.1.0 (file:///Users/PFJ/Dropbox/Rust/Chapter%204%
20-%20Recursion/Code/semicolon_block)
     Running `target/debug/semicolon_block`
x is 5
y is 155
z is ()
Pauls-MacBook-Pro:semicolon_block PFJ$ 
```

In the code example, the line within `fn main` calling `recurse` gives the same result with or without the semicolon, because the Rust runtime doesn't use `main`'s return value for anything.

Summary

In this chapter, we've covered the different types of loops that are available within Rust, as well as gained an understanding of when to use a semicolon and what it means to omit it. We have also considered enumeration and iteration over a vector and an array and how to handle the data held within them.

In the next chapter, we will see why Rust is a good choice for server applications: memory handling.

5
Remember, Remember

One of the main advantages of using Rust over the likes of C is its memory management. For example, C programs will run into buffer overruns and associated undefined behavior if you attempt to write past the end of an array or past an area reserved using `malloc`. Rust protects against most of these problems without compromising on efficiency.

In this chapter, we will delve into how Rust handles memory and will cover the following topics:

- Understanding the memory system used within Rust
- How it can go wrong if you're not careful
- Looking at pointers, references, stack overflows, and preventing crashes
- Allocating and freeing up memory

Let's start at the beginning

In `Chapter 2`, *Variables*, I briefly mentioned how data is stored within memory, and I said that non-compound types, such as `i32`, are stored on the stack, whereas, the likes of `String`, `Vector<T>`, types, and such are stored on the heap.

By default, Rust stores data on the stack, as it's incredibly fast. There are drawbacks though. The stack is limited in size and the allocation only lasts for the lifetime of the function.

The question is, how much memory does a function take?

The stack frame

The stack frame is a term you may have come across. It is the amount of memory allocated to a function, which is used to store all of the local variables and function parameters. In the following snippet, the stack frame will be large enough to store the two `int` values and the single `float32` type:

```
fn main()
{
    let a = 10;
    let b = 20;
    let pi = 3.14f32;
}
```

Once `main` has exited, the stack frame allocated on entry will be released. The beauty of both the allocation and deallocation is that they are carried out without the user needing to do anything. The amount of memory can also be computed ahead of time, as the compiler knows which local variables are in use. This, again, gives a speed increase.

For every positive, there is a downside: the values stored only exist for the lifetime of the method.

What is meant by the stack?

The simplest way to think about the stack is to consider memory as a series of boxes. For these examples, think of the boxes in groups of four: the function name, the address, the variable name, and the value. Here's a `main` function with a single local variable:

```
fn main()
{
    let i = 32;
}
```

The stack boxes will look like this:

Function name	Address	Variable name	Value
main	0	i	32

A slightly different example is as follows:

```
fn second()
{
    let a = 32;
    let b = 12;
}
fn main()
{
    let d = 100;
}
```

Here, we will have two unconnected stack boxes. Since the second function is never called, we never actually allocate memory on the stack for it. The memory allocations are therefore exactly same as in the first example.

Our third example is where we have the main function call to the second function; in this case, we actually reserve memory for the second function:

```
fn second()
{
    let a = 32;
    let b = 12;
}
fn main()
{
    let d = 100;
    second();
}
```

In terms of our stack boxes, we have the following:

Function name	Address	Variable name	Value
second	2	a	32
	1	b	12
main	0	d	100

The variable from the main function has the address of 0 as it is from the top frame-the frame that calls the other function. The value for the address is purely for this example; it can be anywhere and, typically, different types require a different amount of the stack to hold them. For instance, if the number type is 4 bytes in length, the address will be the base address of the stack to store d, then the address + 4 for b, and finally the address + 8 for a.

Once `foo` has returned, the stack reverts to this:

Function name	Address	Variable name	Value
main	0	d	100

As soon as the `main` function has finished, the stack is empty.

This stacking continues for as many different functions as the application has, and they always work in the same way.

Let's consider the heap

As already discussed, the heap is typically used for complex types. The stack frame model can still be used, but it will need modifying, as the stack will need to point to the base address of the complex type on the heap.

Let's construct a stack frame for the following piece of code:

```
fn main()
{
    let f - 42;
    let my_ids: Vec<i64> = Vec::with_capacity(5);
}
```

Function name	Address	Variable name	Value
main	1	f	42
	0	my_ids	(an instance of Vector)

Space is allocated correctly for `f`, but `my_ids` is different; it is a `Vector<i64>` with pre-allocated space for five `i64s` values. While the vector itself is stored in the stack, its contents are allocated in the heap.

Values in the heap are considered to be more persistent than those in the stack. That means, unlike values in the stack, their lifetime does not have to be as short as the block's they were defined in.

Deallocation

Unlike when memory is freed up on the stack, when you deallocate memory from the heap, you end up with holes in the heap. These are empty and can be reallocated to other variables. As with anything to do with memory, the reallocation is handled by the OS.

Deallocation is handled automatically by Rust with a style typically called **Resource acquisition is initialization**. This confusingly named concept means that resources (such as heap memory, but also other things such as file pointers) are allocated during object creation and released during object destruction. Object destruction in Rust happens when the binding goes out of scope. If you need to define custom destructors for your own objects, you can implement the `std::ops::Drop()` trait. It contains a single method, `drop`, which gets called when your object loses its last binding.

What about functions with arguments?

Consider the following piece of code:

```
fn main()
{
    let a = 32;
    let b = &a;
}
```

We have created two variable bindings, with the second one (b) pointing at the address for a. The b variable doesn't contain the value of the a variable, but it points to the position a is held at, from which it can obtain a value (in other words, the value of b is borrowed from a).

In terms of our stack diagram, we have this:

Function name	Address	Variable name	Value
main	1	b	→ address 0
	0	a	32

If we have a function call another function, but with a parameter, our stack will look slightly different:

```
fn second(i: &i32)
{
    let c = 42;
    println!("{}", *i);
}

fn main()
{
    let a = 32;
    let b = &a;
    second(b);
}
```

Function name	Address	Variable name	Value
	3	c	42
second	2	i	→ address 0
	1	b	→ address 0
main	0	a	32

The i binding points to address **0** and the b variable points to address **0**, and this is the parameter being passed to second.

We can use this stack method to think about memory for a complex situation if you like.

Static memory allocation

While we have the stack and heap, Rust also has another type of memory allocation, that is, statically allocated memory. This is not allocated at runtime, but moves into memory with the program's code before the program is run.

The likes of static and const variables are good examples of static allocations.

Static memory allocation has the same lifetime as that of the application.

Garbage collecting time and ownership

If you're used to any of the .NET languages, you'll be more than accustomed to the **garbage collector** (**GC**). Essentially, when all references to an object have gone out of scope, the object's heap allocation is freed up by the garbage collector. The garbage collector comes around every once in a while, basically checks through the whole space of allocated memory to see if something isn't used anymore, and removes such content from memory; in other words, the garbage left behind by a deallocated pointer is collected and removed.

Rust has a primitive garbage collector in the form of a reference counted container, `Rc<T>`. For most cases, it's not required though, as Rust uses a system known as **ownership for allocation**.

Up to this point, when we created a variable, we created variables that mostly live on the stack. These have a very short life span. When we create an object that lives on the heap, we create a single variable that points to it, but then we can have any number of objects point to it, or even through a copy of the pointer, have the copy become the base and free up the original. It gets messy and deallocation of the heap memory can lead to a variety of memory issues.

We can wrap any type in a generic container, `Box<T>`. This creates an owned pointer in Rust, which can only have a single owner, and when that pointer goes out of scope, the memory is automatically freed. In this way, Rust prevents a large number of the problems that we see in other languages. The point of this owned box is that we can hand out the box to other functions, thus being able to return heap allocated variables.

An owned pointer example

Consider the following piece of code:

```
struct MyRectangle
{
    x: i32,
    y: i32,
    length: i32,
    breadth: i32,
}

fn allocate_rect()
{
    let x: Box<MyRectangle> = Box::new (MyRectangle {x: 5, y: 5,
length: 25, breadth:15});
}
```

The x variable is the single owner of the `my_rectangle` object on the heap. As soon as `allocate_rect()` is complete, the memory on the heap allocated to x is freed, since the last owner is gone.

The single owner is enforced by the compiler. The following example demonstrates transferring ownership. Once the transfer is complete, the original cannot be used again:

```
fn swap_around()
{
    let my_rect: Box<MyRectangle> = Box::new(MyRectangle{x:5, y:5,
length:25, breadth:15});
    let dup_rect = my_rect; // dup_rect is now the owner
    println!("{}", dup_rect.x);
    println!("{}", my_rect.x); // won't work - use of moved value
}
```

Comparison to C

Consider the following C code:

```
void myFunction()
{
    int *memblock = malloc(sizeof(int));
    *memblock = 256;
    printf("%d\n", *memblock);
    free(memblock);
}
```

Here's what the preceding code does:

1. The `int` line allocates a block of memory large enough to store an integer value. The `memblock` variable will be in the stack, and the block of memory it points to will be in the heap.
2. A value `256` is placed at the location pointed to by x.
3. The value of the memory location pointed to by x is printed out.
4. The memory allocated to `memblock` is deallocated.

This works well, but has the following three major drawbacks:

- Once the memory is deallocated, it is still entirely possible to use `memblock`. Should you try to do this, the application will exhibit undefined behavior; most likely, the application will just quit, but there is also a chance that it will corrupt memory, which will cause a system crash. The compiler will make no attempt to warn you that you've done this, as it assumes you know what you're doing.
- If you allocate a type larger than what was placed into the `sizeof`, this will also give rise to undefined behavior. You are essentially trying to put a quart into a pint pot.
- If `free` is not called, the memory remains reserved, even though nothing points to it anymore, which leads to memory leaks.

You can perform something similar in Rust but, as we'll see, Rust prevents this undefined behavior automatically:

```
fn myMemory()
{
    let memblock: Box<i64> = Box::new(256);
    println!("{}", memblock);
}
```

There are a number of differences between the C and Rust code versions. They are as follows:

- In C, you allocate heap memory with the `malloc` function. In Rust, we use an owned pointer via the `Box<T>` generic.
- The call to `malloc` in C returns an `int` pointer (`int *`). In Rust, a smart pointer (`Box<T>`) is returned, in this case to an `i64`. A smart pointer is called smart as it controls when the object is freed. This can be when the pointer goes out of scope without the pointer being given away. Rust keeps track of objects and how to clean the memory up.

Another useful smart pointer type is the reference counted pointer, `Rc<T>`. This generic type allows the sharing of the data inside it over multiple locations. It works so that whenever the `Rc` binding gets cloned, a reference count is incremented. Whenever such a binding gets deallocated, the reference count is decremented. Only when the reference count reaches zero is the underlying value deallocated. Note that `Rc<T>` works only in single-threaded scenarios.

It is used like this:

```
// 05/rc-1/src/main.rs
use std::rc::Rc;

fn main()
{
    let memblock: Rc<i64> = Rc::new(256);
    // allocate space on the heap and assign
    secondMethod(memblock.clone());
    // clone a new reference counted pointer and pass it on to the
method
    println!("{}", memblock);
    // output the value
} // free memory here

fn secondMethod(memblock: Rc<i64>)
{
    println!("In secondMethod and memblock is {}", memblock);
    let secMemblock: Rc<i64> = memblock.clone();
    // yet another reference counted pointer to memblock
}
// secMemblock goes out of scope, but the memory is not deallocated
```

In this code, we make several clones of the reference counted pointer. At the peak (on the second line of the `secondMethod` function), we have a total of three pointers to the underlying heap. When we leave `secondMethod`, the pointer allocated via the `secMemBlock` variable gets destructed. Then the `memBlock` clone gets deallocated. Finally, when we exit the main function, the last pointer goes away and the heap memory is deallocated.

Let's revisit some old code

Back in `Chapter 4`, *Conditions, Recursion, and Loops,* we had some code that looked like this:

```
let x = 2;
let y =
    {
        let x_squared = x * x;
        let x_cube = x_squared * x;
        x_cube + x_squared + x
    };
```

It was explained that what it did was assign the result of x_cube + x_squared + x to y. If, outside of that, we attempted to access either x_squared or x_cubed, then we wouldn't be able to, as they only existed within the scope of that calculation for y.

Consider, then, what would happen if we made y a reference and tried to point it to a temporary value:

```
// 05/refs-1/src/main.rs
fn main() {
    let x = 2;
    let y: &i32;
    {
        let x_squared = x * x;
        let x_cube = x_squared * x;
        y = &(x_cube + x_squared + x);
        // this value goes away after this line
    };
    println!("Y = {}", *y);
}
```

We are assigning y to the value of a variable that only exists in a small scope (the temporary unnamed value of the computation), then we're trying to access that value giving rise to undefined behavior. As we've seen, the Rust compiler will do everything it can to prevent this sort of error. In this case, the compiler keeps track of each and every reference and fails to build if a reference lasts longer than the pointer in use.

Let's not race ahead!

As with anything to do with memory, we do have times where memory is shared between pointers. Typically, when we write an application, we don't consider that, at any given time, there may be multiple threads running at the same time, and while we can fairly accurately predict what will happen by following the flow, we can sometimes face an issue known as a race condition. Quite simply, we don't know which condition will *hit* first.

Let's look at the following example:

```
// 05/threads-1/src/main.rs
use std::thread;
use std::rc::Rc;

struct MyCounter
{
    count: i32
}
```

```
fn wont_work()
{
    let mut counter = Rc::new(MyCounter {count: 0});
    thread::spawn(move || // new thread
    {
        counter.count += 1;
    });
    println!("{}", counter.count);
}
```

This won't compile because the compiler doesn't know which thread will be 0 or 1, as they both attempt to access `counter` at the same time. In Rust terms, `counter` gets moved to the inner thread, which means that it cannot be accessed anywhere else. Reference counting via the `Rc` type does not help here, because it's not thread-safe.

Stop the race...

How can this error be avoided?

There's another reference counted type with an incredibly cool name: Atomic RC. Atomicity, in this case, refers to non-divisible actions and/or containers, which means that they are thread-safe. Also, we'll need to pair the `Arc` type with a `Mutex` to allow us to lock the data for access. Here's the full code for a threaded implementation:

```
// 05/threads-2/src/main.rs
use std::thread;
use std::sync::{Arc, Mutex};

struct MyCounter
{
    count: i32
}

fn wont_work()
{
    let counter = Arc::new(Mutex::new(MyCounter {count: 0}));
    let another_counter = counter.clone();
    thread::spawn(move || // new thread
    {
        let mut counter = another_counter.lock().expect("Locking of
cloned counter failed");
        counter.count += 1;
    });
    println!("{}", counter.lock().unwrap().count);
}
```

Usually, this code will print 0 because the print method tends to be reached before the mutation in the thread takes place.

Summary

As far as memory handling is concerned, Rust does a lot for the developer and virtually ensures that it is impossible to run into the same form of issues as found in C. Freeing up memory from the heap is automatic, and there is even protection when using pointers by having unique and multiple protected pointers.

In the next chapter, we will have some respite from learning and see how you can put what we have covered into your own applications.

6
Creating Your Own Rust Applications

We're now roughly half-way through the book and, rather than just continuing, this chapter has a number of tasks for you to attempt. Having a go at them will help reinforce what we have covered so far.

In order to complete these, you will need to create the code as a full project using Cargo, as shown in Chapter 1, *Introducing and Installing Rust*. If you get stuck, possible solutions are included in the source code directory.

Project 1 - let's start with some math

Analyzing of data is very important, and knowing how to produce a straight-line relationship is often of great importance. You will need to construct a couple of functions that will work out something known as a linear regression analysis.

Requirements

The following is a brief list of requirements for our project:

- Data will come from two vectors and will be floating point numbers
- The answers will only be stored in main and displayed from there
- The two vectors must have the same number of elements

Supplied data

The data required for this project is in the `Chapter 6` folder, `Projects/MathsData.txt`. The content of the file should be used within the application (copy and paste). If the data sets do not have the same number of elements, remove elements from the end of the set with the larger number of elements.

Let's look at the math required:

- **The equation of a straight line**:

  The equation is very simple:

  $y = mx + c$, where m is the gradient and c is the intercept on the y axis

- **Gradient of the regression line**:

  The equation is as follows:

  $$m = \frac{\sum y_i \sum x_i - n \sum x_i y_i}{\sum x_i^2 - n \sum x_i^2}$$
  >

  This may look hairy but it's quite simple, so long as the following rule is remembered:

  $\sum x^2$ is not equal to $(\sum x)^2$

So, what is the difference?

$\sum x^2$ means that it is the sum of x^2 while $(\sum x)^2$ is the sum of x squared. Let's consider the following code as an example:

x	1	2	3	4	5
x2	$(12 + 22 + 32 + 42 + 52) = 55$				
(x)2	$(1 + 2 + 3 + 4 + 5)2 = 152 = 225$				

To save time at this point, it is worth performing the following calculations:

- xy for each set, followed by Σxy for each
- $\Sigma x, \Sigma y, \Sigma x^2, (\Sigma x)^2, \bar{x}$ (the average of x), $\bar{y}$ (the average of the y values)

The data is needed for the regression gradient and intercepts on the y value. After that is performed, it is simply a case of plugging in the numbers.

For example, $\sum y = 5.8907$, $\sum x = 5$, $\sum x^2 = 7.5$, $(\sum x)^2 = 25$, $n = 4$, $\sum xy = 8.8528$

$$m = \frac{\sum y_i \sum x_i - n \sum x_i y_i}{\sum x_i^2 - n \sum x_i^2}$$

$$= \frac{(5.8907 * 5) - (4 * 8.8528)}{25 - (4 * 7.5)}$$

$$= \frac{29.4535 - 35.4112}{25 - 30}$$

$$= \frac{-5.9577}{-5}$$

$$= 1.1915$$

Moreover, none of the math from here on in is any harder than that.

- **Getting the intercepts**:

    We already have the formula for the intercept on the y axis (c) by the equation, which is as follows:

$$c = \frac{\sum x_i \sum x_i y_i - \sum y_i \sum x_i^2}{\sum x_i^2 - n \sum x_i^2}$$

Again, using the same data as earlier, the numbers slot in and give an answer of -0.0167.

Now, this is the intercept on y; however, we want the intercept on the x axis as well. To do this, we can say that we want to know the value of x when y = 0. The equation of the straight line is $y = mx + c$; therefore, to get x by itself, the equation will be as follows:

$$\frac{0 - c}{m} = x$$

Simple!

- **Deviation must be known**:

There are two more factors to be considered with the regression analysis-the standard deviation (better known as the error in the line) and the r^2 value (the correlation coefficient; in other words, how good a straight line the line really is).

The two equations are a tad more difficult than before, but not by much.

First off, some more calculations will cover the standard deviation and the r^2 calculations.

For the standard deviation, we will need to know $(y_{expt} - y_{calc})^2$. This can be done in line, as follows:

y_{expt} is the value from your experiment, y_{calc} can be read as mx + c (all three are known). Therefore, if we just plug in the numbers then square the result, we end up with $(y_{expt} - y_{calc})^2$. These numbers are then added together to give $\Sigma(y_{expt} - y_{calc})^2$.

In the r^2 calculation, we will need to calculate $x_i - \bar{x}y_i\bar{y}$ and then sum the results. This is easy, as are the parts in the denominator.

However, wait a second; there is a common item in both the deviation and r^2 calculation, namely raising to the power ½. This is actually just another way of saying a square root.

It is now just a case of plugging in the numbers.

Application output

The application has to output the following information:

- Number of elements in each vector
- If the number of elements in vector are not the same, output the value(s) removed and from which vector is removed from
- The equation of the straight line
- Intercepts on the X and Y axis
- The standard deviation on the data
- The r^2 value

Project 2 - some text manipulation

A palindrome is a word that is spelled the same backwards as it is forward. For example, the word *madam* is a palindrome.

Requirements

The following is a brief list of requirements:

- The application takes a line of text from the keyboard.
- It should fail if the line is blank or contains a non-alphabet character.
- Any text entered should be converted to either lower- or upper-case.
- The word should be tested in a separate function to see if it is a palindrome. If it is, the function should return true; otherwise it should return false.
- The calling function should output whether the inputted text is (or not) a palindrome.

Code notes

The palindrome function should be recursive.

Project 3 – area and volume

This project should help consolidate both testing and documentation for your applications.

You have a simple web service running on a server somewhere. It exists as a test bed for users to send data and receive it back. The service is expecting three strings to be entered, which are as follows:

- Username (string, non-null, must be more than 6 characters, no spaces)
- Password (string, non-null, must be more than 8 characters, no spaces, must have 1 capital, 1 number)
- Command string

The command string is a comma-separated list containing details of whether it is to be a volume or area calculation, the type of shape, and the parameter list.

Shape types

Type	Shape	Type	Shape
0	Circle/Sphere	3	Pentagon
1	Triangle/Pyramid	4	Octagon
2	Rectangle/Box	5	User-defined

Volume or area

For the command string, area is given by true with the volume being false.

User-defined shape

This shape is up to you. It should be a shape is not currently on the list.

Formulae for calculations

You should use the following formulae for the calculations:

Shape	Area	Volume
Circle/sphere (r = radius)	$A = \Pi r^2$	$V = 4/3 \Pi r^3$
Triangle/Pyramid (b = base, h = height, l = length, w = width)	$A = 1/2bh$	$V = \dfrac{lwh}{3}$
Rectangle/Box (l = length, h = height, b = width)	$A = lh$	$V = lbh$
Pentagon (a = side length, h = height)	$A = 1/4\sqrt{5(5 + 2\sqrt{5})a^2}$	$A = 1/4\sqrt{5(5 + 2\sqrt{5})a^2}_h$
Octagon (a and s = side length, h = height)	$A = 2(1 + \sqrt{2})a^2$	$V = (2, s^2, (1 + \sqrt{2}))h/3$

Testing criteria

Consider the following testing criteria:

1. **Command line**: When testing the parameter data, any values as **0** should cause the first test to fail. For the second test, **0** should be replaced with a floating point value of your choice.

    The command line must come in the following format:

    ```
    volume/area, type, params
    ```

    For example, true, 1, 3.1, 33.12, 4.3 is valid; whereas, false, 1, 12 will fail. (It requires two values to be passed in.)

    A command line such as false, 1, 12.1, 13.5, 1.4, 0 will not fail as anything in the parameter list past the required number of parameters for the calculation can be ignored.

    If the command fails, the output should always be **-1**.

2. **Username and password**: The username and passwords have to meet the criteria set out at the start of the puzzle. If they fail, the output should be either Username failed or Password failed. No other reasons are required.

Auto-documentation

Documentation should be generated for each function with the entry and exit parameter clearly stated.

Using regular expressions (regex)

While Rust does come with Regex as its own crate, you are encouraged to create your own method to test string inputs.

Input and output

As with all other examples, this should all be via the standard terminal entry and exit points (read keyboard and monitor). I would suggest three prompts: *username*, *password*, and *command line* as, after each input, it will be simpler to test the input submitted and respond appropriately.

Project 4 – memory

In this project, you are to perform the following:

1. Reserve a 1024-byte block of memory.
2. Fill that block of memory with random characters.
3. Create an array, which is also 1,024 bytes in size.
4. Copy the contents of the memory block into the array.
5. Create a string that is limited to 1,024 bytes and is set using the `capacity` function.
6. Copy the contents of the memory block into the string.

At this point, you may be wondering why we have three identical blocks of memory. The simple reason is that you will now create a piece of code that will rotate each member in turn 3 times using a simple left-bit rotation and then 3 times to the right.

Bitwise rotation

Bitwise rotation is performed in Rust using the << and >> operators.

For example, if we have a variable called x that is rotated 3 to the left, we will write x << 3 with 3 to the right being x >> 3.

Say we have $x = 01101001$, x << 3 will be 01001000 and x >> 3 will be 00001101.

Rotation caveat

While we can simply have x << 3, what we need for this puzzle is to perform a single rotation 3 times, (so it is actually x << 1, x << 1, x << 1).

Output

It is not expected that the values you started off with will be the values you ended up with (if you shift too far, the empty spaces in the byte are filled with 0's). You should be able to find how many bytes have a value of 0. You should display this at the end.

Summary

Trying these four different types of programming challenge should have helped firm up the knowledge you have gained from the first half of the book. In the next half, we'll be covering more advanced topics and will continue to explore the strength and flexibility that Rust can provide.

7
Matching and Structures

On top of the primitive variables and generics, which we will come to in `Chapter 9`, *Introducing Generics, Impl, and Traits*, Rust is capable of storing groups of different types of variables in a `struct` construct that may be familiar to those who have developed in the C family of languages. There's also a related concept called **enumerations** for creating types with alternating options. If that is not enough, Rust can combine these in its powerful pattern-matching code.

In this chapter, we will cover the following topics:

- Learning how to use and manipulate `struct` data types
- Understanding tuples and the **tuple struct** hybrid
- Creating and using enums
- Understanding and applying the basics of patterns and matching

Structs 101

For this chapter, I am going to ask you to imagine the following scenario. I have a house. My house has a certain number of rooms and each room has a name. Each room has one or more doors and windows and a carpet (with a color), and the rooms have a width and length. We will use structs and enums to model all this.

Structs in Rust are very common; they are used in many facets of the language and are useful to understand and use. In terms of the house example, we'll see how useful they can be.

Variables, variables everywhere

Let's look at the house and create some variables to describe it, as well as types. Start with the house, which can be considered the most basic of objects. We will need only to model the number of rooms it has:

```
number_of_rooms: i32
```

Let's consider rooms next.

Each room will have a number of properties. Is it upstairs or downstairs, assuming it's a two-level house? Number of doors. Number of windows. Types of windows. Do the window have curtains? Wood or carpet floor covering? Color of the carpet. Room name. Does it have a wardrobe/closet? Room width. Room length. You can go deeper than that, but this will do for now.

As variables, these will be as follows:

```
is_upstairs: bool
number_of_doors: i32
number_of_windows: i32
window_type: String
has_curtains: bool // true = yes
wood_or_carpet: bool // true = carpet
carpet_color: String
room_name: String
has_wardrobe: bool // true = yes
room_width: f32
room_height: f32
```

There is no reason why you can't define these as discrete variables; however, as they are properties that describe a feature within the house or room, why not group them as we already have? This is where a struct type comes in useful.

The structure of a struct

A struct type consists of three parts: the keyword struct, the struct name, and the variables it holds. Let's consider the following command as an example:

```
struct MyStruct
{
    foo: i32,
    bar: f32,
}
```

It is important to note that, unlike normal variable definitions, a comma follows directly after the variable type and not a semicolon.

For our example, we can define two `struct` types, one for the room and one for the house, as follows:

```
struct Room
{
    is_upstairs: bool,
    number_of_doors: i32,
    number_of_windows: i32,
    window_type: String,
    has_curtains: bool,
    wood_or_carpet: bool,
    carpet_color: String,
    room_name: String,
    has_wardrobe: bool,
    room_width: f32,
    room_height: f32,
}
```

Our house will therefore be as follows:

```
struct House
{
    room:... um...
}
```

A `struct`, while a special type of variable, is still a variable, and as such as a type; a `struct`. We can therefore assign it the same way as we can any other variable type:

```
struct House
{
    room: Room,
}
```

This is fine if we have a house with a single room! We can define an array of rooms, but then that means we will have a fixed number of rooms. Instead, we will define it as the type used within a vector:

```
struct House
{
    rooms: Vec<Room>
}
```

We created two special types of variable that we can declare and access as we would with any other variable. If we look at the room definition, we can break the structure down further; but why would we want to do that?

Smaller is better

There is an argument that the smaller you make the parent structure, the easier it becomes to manage. This is true, but let's look at it in a different way. As it stands, we have a couple of what can be described as objects in their own right within that structure. Here, an object is something that will have its own properties. Let's look at the window.

A window has a size—width and height; it has a type—sash, for instance; it has blinds or curtains, and the blinds/curtains have a color. The window may also have a lock. It may also be a single or double window and the opening may be at the top or side.

There is also no reason why there should only be a single window. If there is more than one window, then we will need to define our window multiple times. Therefore, it makes more sense to define our window and reference that back as a vector in the main structure.

Before that, though, we said the window will have a size (width, length). Each room will have a size and, probably, so will many other things within the house; therefore, we will remove the size and have that as its own `struct`.

Therefore, we have this following `struct` for the window:

```
struct Area
{
    width: f32,
    length: f32,
}

struct Window
{
    window_area: Area,
    window_type: String,
    has_blinds: bool,
    curtain_color: String,
    has_lock: bool,
    top_open: bool,
    single_window: bool,
}
```

This, back in the parent `struct`, will transform into the following:

```
struct Room
{
    is_upstairs: bool,
    number_of_doors: i32,
    window: Vec<Window> ,
    wood_or_carpet: bool,
    carpet_color: String,
    room_name: String,
    has_wardrobe: bool,
    room_area: Area,
}
```

We can carry on doing this for anything else in the room, including a `struct` variable for furniture, as well as possibly reducing the size for carpet—what you do with it is up to you. For now, we'll keep it at this level.

Accessing a struct

In order to access a `struct` variable, we will need to create a variable that can access it:

```
let mut room = Room { is_upstairs: true,
  number_of_doors: 1, wood_or_carpet: true, carpet_color: "Red",
  room_name: "Bedroom 1", has_wardrobe: true };
```

The code for this section is in the `07/simplestruct` folder in the supporting code bundle of this book.

We have not defined all of the variables within that structure, which, for now, is fine, as they still need to be defined before the code will compile. The variable is mutable since we want to change its contents later.

To access one of the members of the `struct`, we will use the dot notation. In this case, we can have the following:

```
println!("Bedroom {} has {} door", room.room_name,
  room.number_of_door);
```

Defining the child structures

We have two types of `struct`—parent and child. Here, the `struct` of `Room` is the parent and it has two children: the window definition and room size. They are very different beasts as the window definition is a `Vec` type, while the other is just a `struct` type.

For the room area, we can use the following when creating an instance of the room type:

```
room_area: Area {width: 2.3f32, length: 4.3f32}
```

We are defining `room_area`, for which we will then define an inline variable which will act as the pointer to the area structure and, finally, create the size of the room. This is accessed using the following code snippet:

```
println!("The room width is {}m by {}m", room.room_area.width,
room.room_area.length);
```

Finally, we have to define the vector of Windows.

This is done in a very similar way to how we define any other vector, which is as follows:

```
window: vec![
        Window {
            window_area: Area {width: 1.3f32, length: 1.4f32},
            window_type: "Main".to_owned(),
            has_blinds: true,
            curtain_color: "Blue".to_owned(),
            has_lock: false,
            top_open: true,
            single_window: true,
        },
        Window {
            window_area: Area {width: 0.9f32, length: 1.1f32},
            window_type: "Small".to_owned(),
            has_blinds: true,
            curtain_color: "Blue".to_owned(),
            has_lock: false,
            top_open: true,
            single_window: true,
        }
```

We will then add a few more `println!` lines to show we have some data:

```
println!("The room width is {}m by {}m", room.room_area.width,
room.room_area.length);
let ref window_two = room.window[1];
println!("Window 2 is {}m by {}m and has {} curtains",
```

```
window_two.window_area.width, window_two.window_area.length,
window_two.curtain_color);
```

When compiled, the code produces the following result:

```
simplestruct — -bash — 80×5
    Running `target/debug/simplestruct`
Bedroom Bedroom 1 has 1 door
The room width is 2.3m by 4.3m
Window 2 is 0.9m by 1.1m and has Blue curtains
Pauls-MacBook-Pro:simplestruct PFJ$
```

We have very quickly, and simply, created a multi-level structure.

Multi-file version

If you look at the source code in the `simplestruct` file, you'll find the structures at the start with the code under it. There is nothing wrong with that, but after a while, it becomes cumbersome, especially if we have a lot of structures and enumerations.

To remove this problem, we can split the structures and code over two files.

However, before we build the code, we will have to provide the `main.rs` file with some sort of pointer to the structures. We can do this in one of three ways. The simplest is to use the `include!` macro:

```
include!("structs.rs");
```

 The source for this section is in the `Chapter 7/multifile` folder, present in the supporting code bundle provided for this book.

This just inserts the contents of the file in the place of the macro call, so it's not the most elegant way and completely sidesteps Rust's module system. So let's look at a better way.

The better way is to reference the module using the following snippet:

```
mod structs;
use structs::*;
```

This can lead to a large number of issues, the biggest being the protection level, `public` or `private`. When compiled like this, many errors, such as the following example, occur:

```
                      multifile — -bash — 80×6
src/main.rs:26:9: 34:10        run `rustc --explain E0451` to see a detailed expl
anation
src/main.rs:27:26: 27:62 error: field `width` of struct `structs::Area` is priva
te [E0451]
src/main.rs:27              window_area: Area {width: 0.9f32, length: 1.1f32},
                                          ^~~~~~~~~~~~~~~~~~~~~~~~~~~~~~~~~~~~~~~~
```

The error will indicate that, though the structure is `public`, the fields within it aren't, so they can't be accessed. The solution is to make all of the fields `public`.

Private versus public fields

By default, all fields within a `struct` are `private` to the module it is created in. This has its uses; for example, if you want to protect a value within the `struct`, you can make it only accessible via a `read`/`write` function, as shown in the following example:

```
// readwrite.rs
pub struct RWData
{
    pub X: i32,
    Y: i32
}

static mut rwdata: RWData = RWData {X: 0, Y: 0};

pub fn store_y(val: i32)
{
    unsafe { rwdata.Y = val; }
}

pub fn new_y() -> i32
{
    unsafe { rwdata.Y * 6 }
}

// main.rs
mod readwrite;
use readwrite::*;

fn main() {
```

```
    store_y(6);
    println!("Y is now {}", new_y());
}
```

 The code for this section is in the `07/readwrite` folder, present in the supporting code bundle provided for this book.

When we build and run this, we will get the following output:

```
readwrite --- -bash --- 80×5
src/readwrite.rs:16      rwdata.Y * 6
src/readwrite.rs:17 }
    Running `target/debug/readwrite`
Y is now 36
Pauls-MacBook-Pro:readwrite PFJ$
```

Structs 102

While we have defined our own structs, we also have access to a structure known as a unit-like `struct`. Unlike our own structs, we can see the likes of the following:

```
struct someStruct;
let x = someStruct;
```

They have nothing after them—no fields defined. These are not the same as the ones we defined, so how do they work?

To understand how they work, we need to understand a tuple `struct` and, in order to understand those, we need to know what a tuple is.

Tuples

Here are two ways to initialize a tuple:

```
let tup = (3, "foo");
let tup: (i32, &str) = (3, "foo");
```

On the first line, we let local type inference work and just declare what is inside the tuple. Rust will figure out the types. On the second line, we declare the types explicitly.

We can have as many (or as few) elements in the list as they are, in fact, an ordered list of a fixed size.

As with other variable types, we can assign one tuple to equal another as long as they contain the same types and number of parameters (arity). For example, the following have the same types and arity and so can be used to assign to each other:

```
let mut change = (1.1f32, 1);
let into = (3.14f32, 6);
change = into;
```

The following wouldn't be allowed as the types don't match, even though the arity does:

```
let mut change = (1.1f32, 1);
let into = (1, 3.14f32);
```

Using a tuple to define a variable

Let's consider the following:

```
let test = 1i32;
```

We created a variable called `test` that has the value 1 of type `i32` bound to it (binding was discussed in `Chapter 5`, *Remember, Remember*). How can we do something similar with a tuple? So far, we've done the following:

```
let test = (1, 4f32);
```

We bound `test` to a tuple containing two values: `(i32, f32)`.

Tuple indexing

To get at the `f32` value, we will have to use tuple indexing. This is very similar to indexing an array, but we replace the following snippet:

```
let t = someArray[3];
```

We use the following snippet instead:

```
let t = test.1
```

As with array indexes, the tuple indexes range from 0 to n−1.

Destructuring with let

To avoid using a tuple index, Rust has a way to destructure a tuple. This is very similar to a normal `let` statement, except we will define multiple variable names at once:

```
let (one, two, three) = (1, 2, 3);
```

If there are the same number of names on the left as there are arguments on the right, Rust will break these up internally to create three bindings at once.

We now have three bindings and can access them as we would any other variable:

```
let (one, two, three) = (1, 2, 3);
println!("One = {}", one); // outputs One = 1
```

Tuple structs – the hybrid of two

Consider a `struct` with three fields. It will have a name for the `struct` type and the three fields with their types:

```
struct Test
{
    drink: bool,
    number: i32,
    price: f32
}
```

Let's consider what this actually is and if we can we not rewrite this as follows:

```
let Test: (bool, i32, f32) = (false, 4, 1.55);
```

Well, we can, but we will now run into how to access the members of the tuple. We will also run into assigning one tuple to another. You can't really define two structs, which are identical in everything other than the `struct` type name, and then assign the second `struct` type to the first.

To get around this, Rust has the tuple `struct` hybrid. It contains the `struct` type but then assigns the fields as a tuple:

```
struct TestOne (f32, i8, &str);
struct TestTwo (f32, i8, &str);
```

We now have the flexibility of a tuple, but with the protection of the `struct`. Despite the arity being the same and the types inside the struct being the same, they are different types.

As with a regular tuple, we can access the members of the tuple `struct` in the same way:

```
let i = TestOne.1;
```

The single element tuple struct

At this point, you're probably wondering whether there are any uses for a tuple `struct` over a standard `struct`. One of the uses is when the tuple `struct` has a single element. Here, we are able to create a variable based on the tuple. It's similar to a destructured tuple in appearance:

```
struct MyPi(f32);
fn main()
{
    let my_pi = MyPi(22f32 / 7f32);
    let MyPi(pi) = my_pi;
    println!("pi = {}", pi);
}
```

 The source for this section is in the `07/newtype` folder, present in the supporting code bundle provided for this book.

This produces the following output when compiled and run:

```
newtype — -bash — 80×6

   Compiling newtype v0.1.0 (file:///Users/PFJ/Dropbox/Rust/Chapter%207%20-%20St
ructs%20Enums/Code/newtype)
     Running `target/debug/newtype`
pi = 3.142857
Pauls-iMac:newtype PFJ$
```

This form of assignment is known as a new type pattern; it has allowed the creation of a new type distinct from the contained value.

Back to the unit-like struct

Now that we have an understanding of tuples and the tuple `struct`, we can now look at the unit-like `struct`. This can be considered to be a `struct` with an empty tuple and as with a tuple `struct`, it defines a new type.

Typically, we will use this in conjunction with a trait or if you don't have any data to store in it.

Enumerations

If are you are used to C, you will be well used to enumerations, for example:

```
enum myEnum {start = 4, next, nextone, lastone=999};
```

This creates an `enum` type that auto-fills `next` and `nextone` to be start + 1 and start + 2 respectively. If the first named parameter has nothing to give an initial value to, it is given the value 0 with everything after it being one larger than the last. They are accessed as `myEnum.nextone`.

An `enum` type in Rust has a very similar structure to a `struct` type, as shown in the following code:

```
enum MyEnum
{
    TupleType(f32, i8, &str),
    StructType { varone: i32, vartwo: f64 },
    NewTypeTuple(i32),
    SomeVarName
}
```

As with C though, an `enum` is a single type, but the value of the `enum` can match any of its members.

Accessing enumeration members

Given the possibility of the contents of a Rust `enum`, you may be thinking that accessing one of the members within the enumeration may not be the simplest of tasks. Thankfully, it is, as an `enum` variable is sometimes referred to as a *scopable* variable. For example, if we wanted to access members, we could use the following:

```
enum MyFirstEnum
{
    TupleType(f32, i8, String),
    StuctType {varone: i32, vartwo: f64},
    NewTypeTuple(i32),
    SomeVarName
}
```

```
enum MySecondEnum
{
    TupleType(f32, i8, String),
    StuctType {varone: i32, vartwo: f64},
    NewTypeTuple(i32),
}

fn main()
{
    let mut text1 = "".to_owned(); // text1: String
    let mut text2 = "".to_owned(); // text2: String
    let mut num1 = 0f32;
    let value = MyFirstEnum::TupleType(3.14, 1, "Hello".to_owned());
    let value2 = MySecondEnum::TupleType(6.28, 0, "World".to_owned());
    if let MyFirstEnum::TupleType(f,i,s)  = value
    {
        text1 = s;
        num1 = f;
    }
    if let MySecondEnum::TupleType(f,i,s) = value2
    {
        text2 = s;
    }
    println!("{} {} from the {} man", text1, text2, num1)
}
```

 The code for this section is in the `07/enumscope` folder, present in the supporting code bundle provided for this book.

The variables, `value1` and `value2`, are scoped (uses `::`) to `MyFirstEnum` and `MySecondEnum` respectively. When compiled, we will see the following output:

```
                        enumscope — -bash — 115×5
    in expansion of if let expansion
src/main.rs:31:5: 34:6       expansion site
     Running `target/debug/enumscope`
Hello World from the 3.14 man
Pauls-iMac:enumscope PFJ$ 
```

The two questions you should be asking

The code is a bit of head-scratcher. Surely we should have been able to use something similar to the following code?

```
let value = MyFirstEnum::TupleType(3.14, 1, "Hello".to_owned());
```

And then use `value.2` to obtain the string part directly within the `println!` statement, instead of the `if let` construct?

The reason why we can't is that `enum` variants aren't their own type, so as soon as we create the preceding value, above it is immediately lost.

The second question should be: What is the `if let` construct?

In Rust, `if let` is used as a way to perform certain types of pattern-matching.

Patterns and matching

Rust, as we have seen, contains many very powerful facilities. We will now consider two that are often seen, and then double back to examine how we can use the `if let` construct.

Matching

Let's look at a very unpleasant code block and then examine what it means:

```
fn my_test(x: i32) -> String
{
    if x == 1
    {
        return "one".to_owned();
    }
    else if x == 2
    {
        return "two".to_owned();
    }
    else if x == 3
    {
        return "three".to_owned();
    }
    return "not found".to_owned();
}
```

The code takes an i32 parameter and tests to see what it equals. If the condition is met, some text is returned for that number; otherwise, "not found" is returned.

This is a trivial example, but imagine if you're testing against 10 different conditions; the if-else construct will become ugly.

If we were in C, we could use switch/case and Rust can also do something similar, but the keyword is match instead. If we used the match expression, our function would be as follows:

```
fn my_test(x: i32) -> String
{
    let mut t = "".to_owned();
    match x
    {
        1 => t = "one".to_owned(),
        2 => t = "two".to_owned(),
        3 => t = "three".to_owned(),
        _ => t = "not found".to_owned()
    }
    return t;
}
```

In this instance, when x is matched to the value inside of the match expression, t is assigned. If it is not matched (_ => ...), then t is set to be not found. There must be a _ wildcard pattern case within the match. This is down to Rust enforcing exhaustiveness checking. In other words, until the _ wildcard is reached, Rust assumes that there must be other values to attempt to match.

Let's really make the function simple

While the preceding example is fairly compact, we can further reduce the footprint of the code by using match as an expression.

If you're used to ? in C#, you will be familiar with a construct such as the following:

```
var t = SomeCondition == 3 ? "three" : (SomeCondition == 4 ?
  "four" : "not three or four");
```

This means that we can assign t to be three if SomeCondition == 3 else ifSomeCondition == 4, t = four. If this falls through, we can set t as not three or four.

It can get messy. Rust can do the same, only far more cleanly.

In the origin code, we had the following:

```
let mut t = "".to_string();
match x
{
```

We can use `match` as an expression to set the value to be returned:

```
let t = match x
{
    ...
};
return t;
```

Or, more simply, by just returning the result of the match:

```
return match x
{
    ...
};
```

Or even more simply, when we remember that, in Rust, a block returns the result of its last expression when we omit the `;`:

```
fn my_test(x: i32) -> String {
    match x {
        1 => "one".to_owned(),
        2 => "two".to_owned(),
        3 => "three".to_owned(),
        _ => "not found".to_owned()
    }
}
```

Using match with an enum

We have already seen in this chapter how enums can be somewhat tricky to handle. Thankfully, we can use `match` on an `enum`:

```
enum MyFirstEnum
{
    TupleType(f32, i8, String),
    StructType {varone: i32, vartwo: f64},
    NewTypeTuple(i32),
    SomeVarName
}
```

```
fn tuple_type(v: f32, c: i8, st: String) {//code}
fn struct_type(v1: i32, v2: f64) {//code}
fn new_type_tuple(n: i32) {//code}
fn process_varname() {//code}

fn match_enum_code(e: MyFirstEnum)
{
match e {
   MyFirstEnum::SomeVarName => process_varname(),
   MyFirstEnum::TupleType(f,i,s) => tuple_type(f,i,s),
   MyFirstEnum::StructType(v1,v2) => struct_type(v1,v2),
   MyFirstEnum::NewTypeTuple(i) => new_type_tuple(i)
};
}
```

You will notice that in this example, _ is not included. That's because we explicitly match against all the possible choices of the enum, so we don't need a catch-all case. If, for instance, we missed NewTypeTuple, the code would need to include a catch-all:

```
fn match_enum_code(e:MyFirstEnum)
{
match e {
   MyFirstEnum::SomeVarName => process_varname(),
   MyFirstEnum::TupleType(f,i,s) => tuple_type(f,i,s),
   MyFirstEnum::StructType(v1,v2) => struct_type(v1,v2),
   _ => return  // breaks out of the match
};
}
```

Ignoring a parameter with match

It is entirely possible to ignore a parameter within a match construct. Take the following struct:

```
struct Test
{
    answer: i32,
    real_answer: i32,
    score: i32,
}
```

We can use this `struct` within a `match` construct as we can any other type. However, we want to ignore anything after `real_answer`. To do this, we will use the `..` operator. Our match will look like this:

```
fn match_test(t: Test)
{
    match t
    {
        Test {answer: Question::MyAnswer, real_answer:
         Question::RealAnswer, ..} => {...}
    }
}
```

We can also use _ as a parameter (we expect a value, but we don't care what it is):

```
fn match_test(t:Test)
{
    match t
    {
        Test {answer: Question::MyAmswer, real_answer:
         Question::RealAnswer, score:_} => {...}
    }
}
```

You can appreciate that the `match` construct is powerful, but let's see it in action with patterns.

Fall through patterns

Let's say that we want to have a fall through construct in the same way as we would have in C:

```
switch(foo)
{
    case 1:
    case 2: printf("1 and 2\n");
            break;
    case 3: printf("3\n");
            break;
}
```

We can do this in Rust using the | pattern, which is as follows:

```
match foo
{
    1 | 2 => println!("1 and 2"),
    3 => println!("3"),
    _ => println!("anything else")
}
```

Ranges

In a similar way to using |, we can match on a range of values, as follows:

```
match foo
{
    1 ... 10 => println!("Value between 1 and 10"),
    _ => println!("Value not between 1 and 10")
}
```

We can use something similar with `char`, as shown in the following example:

```
match char_foo
{
    'A' ... 'M' => println!("A - M"),
    'N' ... 'Y' => println!("N - Y"),
    'Z' => println!("Z"),
    _ => println!("something else")
}
```

Creating a binding within a match pattern

Sometimes, it is very useful to create a temporary variable within a `match` construct and bind the result of the pattern to it. This is performed using @, as follows:

```
match test
{
    e @ 1 ... 10 => println!("the value is {}", e),
    _ => println!("nothing doing")
}
```

This attempts to match the pattern 1 to 10 to the value of `test`. If it is a match, the value is bound to `t`, which we can then manipulate as we would any other variable.

We can also bind to the variable with a fall through construct as done in the following example:

```
match test
{
    t @ 1 ... 5 | t @ 10 ... 15 => println!("our value for t = {}", t),
    _ => println!("dunno!")
}
```

Let's add an if into the mix

We can include an `if` statement within a `match` pattern, as follows:

```
fn testcode(t: u8)
{
    match t
    {
        1 | 2 if t != 1 => println!("t was not one"),
        1 | 2 if t != 2 => println!("t was not two"),
        _ => println!("")
    }
}
```

Using match with a compound type

A compound type is a type that contains many different types—a `struct` is possibly the simplest example here. The following also applies to enums and tuples.

We can match on a `struct` pattern the same way we can match on any other type of pattern, which is shown in the following example:

```
struct MyStruct
{
    a: i32,
    b: i32
}

fn derp(){
    let mystruct=MyStruct{a:1, b:2};
    match mystruct {
        MyStruct{a, b} => println!("matched the structure"),
        _ => println!("didn't match the structure")
    }
}
```

As described in the matching section, we can ignore parameters in the `struct` pattern match using `..`, or just throw them away using `_`.

And back to if let

You have probably realized now that `if let` is, in actuality, a `match` construct that is just written in a slightly different way.

A `match` construct is as follows:

```
match testmatch
{
    1 => println!("1"),
    _ => println!("not 1")
}
```

The `if let` version would be as follows:

```
if let 1 = testmatch {
    println!("1");
}
 else
 {
    println!("not 1");
}
```

Summary

In this chapter, we saw how Rust deals with some fairly complex types that allow us to create a type which contains many different types, and how handling these compound types can be a mostly painless affair. We have also drawn attention to pitfalls when using enums.

We have examined the structured and flexible approach Rust takes to patterns and matching and the power that simplicity provides to developers.

In the next chapter, we will be looking at something that takes a fair bit of practice to understand and even more to get right—the Rust lifetime system.

8
The Rust Application Lifetime

Rust, as we have seen, is a very stable language. It is also what can be described as a memory-safe language in that, when the code is compiling, the compiler tests the code to ensure that things don't go wrong, such as accessing outside of an array or freeing memory twice.

This is purely down to Rust obeying three key rules—ownership, references (or borrowing, as it's more commonly known), and the application lifetime.

In this chapter, we will discuss and see how the three key facets work to ensure that your Rust application always behaves itself. They are as follows:

- Ownership
- Borrowing
- Lifetime

What are they?

In a nutshell, we can think of the three facets in these terms.

Ownership

When we think of ownership, we inevitably think of possession. I have a MacBook Pro, which I'm writing this text on currently. It is not part of any finance agreement, stolen, borrowed, or on a lease, therefore the ownership of it is mine.

Borrowing

Should I sell or dispose of my computer, I will release the ownership to the next party, or to the recycling facilities. If my son has a DVD that I want to use, I will borrow it from him—he has not released ownership to me, just given it to me for a finite period. He will keep a record, or a reference, that I have it.

Lifetime

This is how long something lasts and, unfortunately, virtually nothing lasts forever. Once the application or ownership ends, the time from taking ownership to removing ownership, which includes the borrowing of something, is considered the lifetime of that object or process.

Let's consider each of these facets in more detail.

Ownership in Rust

In order to appreciate ownership, we will need to take a small detour into compilation abstractions and a very common pitfall.

Abstractions

One aspect of any Rust application that holds it above other applications from other languages is that they are really fast and memory-safe. This is down to an ideal called a **zero-cost abstraction**. An abstraction is a way of hoisting a low-level construct higher, making it easier, safer, and more reliable. These are commonly seen in cross-platform libraries where a user interface has a common abstraction layer, so developers only need to say `var n = new Label {Text = "Hello"};` to create a label for the UI without needing to know what is going on under the hood.

It is usual that abstractions cause some sort of penalties, meaning that code that uses abstractions would run slower or use more memory than corresponding lower-level code. In terms of Rust, these zero-cost abstractions mean that, in terms of computer resources, they cause no penalties. This is normally performed during compilation; the compiler generates the abstractions and executes them. Once done, the compiler will generate the best possible code.

This does have a problem—the compiler will object to code that the developer considers completely fine. This is because, as people, we don't think the same way as a language does, so what we consider as correct ownership is not how Rust considers it. Thankfully, as time goes on, and you use Rust more, this problem becomes far less of one.

Ownership – from the beginning

Let's start by considering a very simple piece of code to help you understand how this works. We have seen the likes of the following plenty of times up to this point:

```
fn my_function()
{
    let mypi = 3.14f32;
}
```

When `my_function` is called (it comes into scope), Rust will allocate memory on the stack to store this value. When the function ends (it goes out of scope), Rust will do an automatic cleanup to deallocate any memory used by `mypi`.

A vector, or anything else that uses the heap, works in a similar way:

```
fn my_second_function()
{
    let myvec = vec![1.1f32, 2.2f32, 3.14f32];
}
```

If you recall from `Chapter 5`, *Remember, Remember*, the vector requires memory both on the heap and on the stack and can be thought of like this:

Function name	Address	Variable name	Value
heap	heap_posn - 1		base_of_vecs
	heap_posn - 2		Vec[1]
my_second_function	0	myvec	heap_posn - 1

This time, when `my_second_function` goes out of scope, not only is the position on the stack cleared, but also the contiguous locations pointed to by `myvec` on the heap.

I've given two examples of variables here for a good reason—the handling is different; a vector takes a generic parameter and these are handled differently to a standard variable type.

It's not quite as simple as this though, and to really understand how things work with ownership, we will really need to consider things on a basic level.

Variable binding

Let's consider the creation of a variable:

```
let myvar = 10i32;
```

We have created a non-mutable variable with the name `myvar`. We will then say that this variable has the value `10` as a 32-bit integer. In other words, if this was in C, it would be as follows:

```
const int myvar = 32;
```

What we have actually done here is create a binding between the variable name and the value. We say that `10i32` is bound to `myvar`. Bindings are very important when it comes to ownership. Rust has a rule that you can only have something bound to something else once.

Let's consider the following snippet as it demonstrates why things go wrong when at the zero-cost abstraction level:

```
let myvec = vec![1i32, 2i32, 3i32];
let myothervec = myvec;
```

Normally, as a developer, you'd look at this and say that `myvec` is bound to a vector of type `i32`, which contains three elements. You'd then assume that `myothervec` is just a copy of the first vector as in the likes of C, C++, and C#; that is what it means. The implementation will vary, but the meaning is the same.

The problem is that, in Rust, what it means is that I have first created `myvec`. When I then say that `myothervec = myvec`, I am actually telling the compiler that the ownership of what `myvec` was bound to has now been given to `myothervec` and therefore `myvec` is out of scope and if (as a developer) I try to do anything with `myvec`, then the compiler is to fail the build.

The following screenshot demonstrates this (it can be found in `Chapter 8/outofscope`). When you attempt to build it, you will get the following results:

```
                          outofscope — -bash — 80×24
    Compiling outofscope v0.1.0 (file:///Users/PFJ/Dropbox/Rust/Chapter%208%20-%2
0Lifecycle/Code/outofscope)
src/main.rs:4:31: 4:36 error: use of moved value: `myvec` [E0382]
src/main.rs:4     println!("myvec[0] = {}", myvec[0]);
                                            ^~~~~~
<std macros>:2:25: 2:56 note:  in this expansion of format_args!
<std macros>:3:1: 3:54 note:   in this expansion of print! (defined in <std macros
>)
src/main.rs:4:5: 4:41 note:    in this expansion of println! (defined in <std macro
s>)
src/main.rs:4:31: 4:36 note:      run `rustc --explain E0382` to see a detailed expla
nation
src/main.rs:3:9: 3:19 note:      `myvec` moved here because it has type `collections:
:vec::Vec<i32>`, which is moved by default
src/main.rs:3       let myothervec = myvec;

src/main.rs:3:9: 3:19 note:      if you would like to borrow the value instead, use a
 `ref` binding as shown:
src/main.rs:       let ref myothervec = myvec;
error: aborting due to previous error
Could not compile `outofscope`.

To learn more, run the command again with --verbose.
Pauls-MacBook-Pro:outofscope PFJ$ ▯
```

We will get a similar sort of issue when a function takes ownership.

The following can be found in 08/function_outofscope:

```
fn transfer_vec(v: Vec<i32>)
{
    println!("v[0] in transfer_vec = {}", v[0]);
}

fn main()
{
    let myvec = vec![1i32, 2i32, 3i32];
    transfer_vec(myvec);
    println!("myvec[0] is: {}", myvec[0]);
}
```

On the first look through, we don't see the obvious transfer of ownership and, usually, when you pass a variable to a function, you don't really consider that as a transfer. In Rust, passing a variable directly to another function is the same as in our first example: the ownership is released from myvec and passed to the function.

To prove this, try to compile the code and you will end up with the following output:

```
Pauls-MacBook-Pro:function_outofscope PFJ$ cargo run
   Compiling function_outofscope v0.1.0 (file:///Users/PFJ/Dropbox/Rust/Chapter%
208%20-%20Lifecycle/Code/function_outofscope)
src/main.rs:12:33: 12:38 error: use of moved value: `myvec` [E0382]
src/main.rs:12     println!("myvec[0] is: {}", myvec[0]);
                                                ^~~~~
<std macros>:2:25: 2:56 note: in this expansion of format_args!
<std macros>:3:1: 3:54 note: in this expansion of print! (defined in <std macros
>)
src/main.rs:12:5: 12:43 note: in this expansion of println! (defined in <std mac
ros>)
src/main.rs:12:33: 12:38 note: run `rustc --explain E0382` to see a detailed exp
lanation
src/main.rs:10:18: 10:23 note: `myvec` moved here because it has type `collectio
ns::vec::Vec<i32>`, which is non-copyable
src/main.rs:10     transfer_vec(myvec);

error: aborting due to previous error
Could not compile `function_outofscope`.

To learn more, run the command again with --verbose.
Pauls-MacBook-Pro:function_outofscope PFJ$ []
```

In other words, it's the same error as earlier.

Stack and heap variables

To understand why we get this problem, we will need to understand in depth how Rust works, and by this I mean at memory level.

Let's start with our variable:

```
let myvar = 32i32;
```

As I've said, in our minds, we will create a `myvar` variable of type `i32` and bind it to the value 32. Rust, on the other hand, does it differently.

Firstly, it identifies that we will need space on the stack for a value that is the size of `i32`.

Next, it copies the value for `32` into that space allocated on the stack.

Lastly, it binds the binding to the position of the stack allocated block to the variable name.

In other words, the complete opposite to how we do it in our minds.

Let's see what happens when we create another binding, like this:

```
let myvartwo = myvar;
```

The compiler moves the binding to where the data sits on the stack for `myvar` and then says that that position (and data) belongs to `myvartwo`. The binding will be transferred. What happens to `myvar` though? Rust won't allow things to *dangle* or allow information to be bound to two different objects. Once the binding is transferred, `myvar` is removed.

The same thing happens if the binding points to something in the heap. Therefore, when we consider `let myvec = vec![1i32, 2i32, 3i32];`, `let myvec = vec![1i32, 2i32, 3i32];` we know how this will work. The compiler knows that it requires space on the heap, enough to hold three elements of type `i32`. These values are copied into the locations and the base address of the contiguous chunk of memory is bound to `myvec`.

Now, let's transfer ownership:

```
let vectwo = myvec;
```

Now, `vectwo` is the only usable binding to the vector on the heap, and `myvec` gets invalidated.

Why is this important?

A very common error in the likes of C# is when you have the following code:

```
var myList = new List<int>{1,2,3,4,5,6};
var dupVar = myList;
dupVar.Remove(4); // 4
foreach(var n in myList)
    Console.WriteLine(n);
```

The output we will get from this may not be as you would expect, which is as follows:

It may be expected that, as we have removed the duplicate from `dupVar`, the `myList` variable should still have all of the numbers it was set to originally. In this code, what is happening is that `dupVar` is known as a copy pointer—we have two variables bound to the same pointer on the stack. While it may not seem that big a deal, we have two variable names that are able to change data. This catches a lot of people out and leads to more memory and content bugs than it is worth.

As Rust only allows one pointer per block, we cannot have the likes of this. Once ownership is transferred, the original bound name can no longer be accessed.

The Copy trait

The code for this section can be found in `08/copyint` and `08/copyf32`.

Rust does have a way to create a copy of the original: the `Copy` trait (traits are covered in `Chapter 10`, *Creating your own Crate*) and all primitives implement `Copy`. If we have something along the lines of `let varone = 1i32;` or `let vartwo = varone;`, then `i32` is a primitive type and the `vartwo` variable will contain a copy of `varone`. Both will have their own allocations on the stack, rather than `vartwo` pointing to `varone`. Ownership will not be changed; the value is duplicated and bound to the new variable.

The code for this section can be found in the `08/copyint` and `08/copyf32` folders in the supporting code bundle provided for this book.

Therefore, we can write the code as follows:

```
fn do_something(number: i32) -> i32
{
    number + 32
}

fn main()
{
    let num = 10i32;
    let numtwo = do_something(num);
    println!("num is: {}", num);
    println!("numtwo is : {}", numtwo);
}
```

The preceding code will give the following output when compiled (numone is an i32 value, which is a primitive, so it makes a copy of itself when passed to do_something with an i32 being returned into numtwo):

```
copyint — -bash — 80×24
Pauls-MacBook-Pro:copyint PFJ$ cargo run
   Compiling copyint v0.1.0 (file:///Users/PFJ/Dropbox/Rust/Chapter%208%20-%20Li
fecycle/Code/copyint)
     Running `target/debug/copyint`
num is: 10
numtwo is : 42
```

The copyf32 example shows the same Copy trait in action but for an f32 primitive.

There must be a way around this.

In a way, we've seen an answer already in many examples used throughout this book—we hand the ownership back; however, as the following code block shows, it can get a bit messy:

```
fn sumprod(v1: Vec<i32>, v2: Vec<i32>) -> (Vec<i32>, Vec<i32>, i32)
{
    let sum = v1.iter().fold(0i32, |a, &b| a + b);
    let product = v2.iter().fold(1i32, |a, &b| a * b);
    return (v1, v2, sum + product); // return ownership
}

fn main()
{
    let vecone = vec![2,3,5];
    let vectwo = vec![3,5];
```

```
    let (vecone, vectwo, ans) = sumprod(vecone, vectwo); // pass ownership
    println!("ans = {}", ans);
}
```

The preceding code will give the following output:

```
🔴 🟡 🟢              handback — -bash — 80×24
Pauls-MacBook-Pro:handback PFJ$ cargo run
   Compiling handback v0.1.0 (file:///Users/PFJ/Dropbox/Rust/Chapter%208%20-%20L
ifecycle/Code/handback)
src/main.rs:13:10: 13:16            unused variable: `vecone`, #[warn(unused_varia
bles)] on by default
src/main.rs:13     let (vecone, vectwo, ans) = sumprod(vecone, vectwo); // pass
ownership

src/main.rs:13:18: 13:24            unused variable: `vectwo`, #[warn(unused_varia
bles)] on by default
src/main.rs:13     let (vecone, vectwo, ans) = sumprod(vecone, vectwo); // pass
ownership

   Running `target/debug/handback`
ans = 25
```

The code for this section can be found in the `Chapter8/handback` folder in the supporting code bundle provided for this book.

Thankfully, Rust does provide a neater way to pass ownership around. Instead of giving ownership, we can borrow ownership.

Borrowing in Rust

Way back in Chapter 2, *Variables*, we referred to something known as a reference and it was said to be a copy of the pointer to some memory location. This is a big part of what is meant by borrowing in Rust.

In our preceding example, we can make use of borrowing. Our code for it is as follows:

```
fn sumprod(v1: &Vec<i32>, v2: &Vec<i32>) -> i32
{
    let sum = v1.iter().fold(0i32, |a, &b| a + b);
    let product = v2.iter().fold(1i32, |a, &b| a * b);
    return sum + product;
}

fn main()
{
    let vecone = vec![2,3,5];
    let vectwo = vec![3,5];
    let ans = sumprod(&vecone, &vectwo);
    println!("ans = {}", ans);
}
```

 The code for this section can be found in the 08/handback folder which can be found in the supporting code bundle of this book.

We will no longer pass ownership, but rather we will pass the reference to the vector. When compiled, we will get the following result:

```
                              borrowing — -bash — 80×24
Pauls-MacBook-Pro:borrowing PFJ$ cargo run
         Running `target/debug/borrowing`
ans = 25
```

Borrow immutability

If we look back to the start of this chapter, I described borrowing as borrowing a DVD from my son. When I take possession of the DVD, I cannot change it, as my son would expect the same DVD back.

The same applies for Rust: the references cannot be changed as they are immutable values. If you think about it, this makes sense. Let me explain.

I have created a `Vec<T>` array type, which is, let's say, eight values long (it doesn't matter what the values are or the type they are). When the binding between the heap and stack is made, it will be of a particular type. If we allow the reference to alter the vector, we will have the same problem as the C# example and so the guarantees can't be assured and the Rust compiler will fail the build. To ensure that the guarantee is kept, Rust simply says that you are unable to change the values borrowed.

Mutable borrows

This is more a writable DVD than a prerecorded one if we use the analogy of borrowing a DVD.

Here, we are using a mutable reference, and we have to be careful how we use these.

The code for this section is in the `08/mutableref1` and `08/mutableref2` folders in the supporting code bundle provided for this book.

In our first example (`mutableref1`), we will create a variable, the reference, do something, and get a new value out:

```
fn main()
{
    let mut mutvar = 5;
    {
        println!("{}", mutvar); // outputs 5
        let y = &mut mutvar; // creates the mutable ref to mutvar
        *y += 1; // adds one to the reference and passes it back in to
mutvar
    }
    println!("{}", mutvar); // outputs 6
}
```

The important line here is `*y += 1;` and, in particular, the `*`, as this means we're directly altering the value of the memory position that the reference points to. When dealing with anything to do with memory, absolute care has to be observed.

The second important point to observe is that we have a set of braces around the code used in the mutable reference. Remove them and everything fails (mutableref2):

```
Pauls-MacBook-Pro:mutableref2 PFJ$ cargo run
   Compiling mutableref2 v0.1.0 (file:///Users/PFJ/Dropbox/Rust/Chapter%208%20-%
20Lifecycle/Code/mutableref2)
src/main.rs:9:20: 9:26 error: cannot borrow `mutvar` as immutable because it is
also borrowed as mutable [E0502]
src/main.rs:9     println!("{}", mutvar); // outputs 6
                                  ^~~~~~
<std macros>:2:25: 2:56 note: in this expansion of format_args!
<std macros>:3:1: 3:54 note: in this expansion of print! (defined in <std macros
>)
src/main.rs:9:5: 9:28 note: in this expansion of println! (defined in <std macro
s>)
src/main.rs:6:22: 6:28 note: previous borrow of `mutvar` occurs here; the mutabl
e borrow prevents subsequent moves, borrows, or modification of `mutvar` until t
he borrow ends
src/main.rs:6              let y = &mut mutvar; // creates mutable reference to mutva
r

src/main.rs:10:2: 10:2 note: previous borrow ends here
src/main.rs:2 {
...
src/main.rs:10 }

error: aborting due to previous error
Could not compile `mutableref2`.
```

The important line is the result of the error; it is saying that you cannot borrow the same item as both mutable and immutable at the same time. It's like saying you can borrow something that can and can't be changed at the same time! Utter nonsense. This is down to borrowing having rules.

The Rust borrowing rules

There are two rules that must be observed with borrowing, which are as follows:

- What you borrow must not outlive the original
- You can have one of the following types of borrow, but never at the same time:
  - One (or more) references of type &T to a resource
  - Only one mutable reference

The first rule makes sense: you can't have the reference outlive where it came from as once where it comes from goes out of scope, it is destroyed and, once destroyed, what are you borrowing exactly?

The second one requires a bit more thought about why it is as it should be and what it is that Rust is trying to achieve.

In this case, Rust is ensuring that something known as a **race condition** occurs (if you are used to writing multithreaded applications, you'll already understand these).

Here, Rust is trying to prevent two references trying to access the same point of memory at the same time. In other words, Rust is trying to prevent a synchronization error.

With non-mutable references, you can have as many as you'd like, as the references can never be written to. With a mutable reference, Rust prevents the problem by allowing just a single reference to be valid.

With this in mind, can we use these rules to fix our code from `mutableref2` in order to do away with the `{}` braces around the mutable reference?

Fixing the problem

Let's examine the code again (I've removed anything from the original that is not required here):

```
let mut mutvar = 5;
let y = &mut mutvar;
*y += 1;
println!("{}", mutvar);
```

When we try and compile, we get the following output returned from the compiler:

```
src/main.rs:9:20: 9:26 error: cannot borrow `mutvar` as immutable because it is
also borrowed as mutable [E0502]
src/main.rs:9       println!("{}", mutvar); // outputs 6
```

We have broken the second rule—you can only have a single mutable or many immutables, never both.

How can we solve this? Let's look back to the original `mutableref1`:

```
fn main()
{
    let mut mutvar = 5;
    {
        println!("{}", mutvar); // outputs 5
        let y = &mut mutvar; // creates mutable reference to mutvar
        *y += 1; // adds 1 and passes result back in to mutvar
    }
    println!("{}", mutvar); // outputs 6
}
```

This works, but why?

Think about the scope

What is actually happening with this code is that we created a new scope for the borrowing section of the code, which passes back in to `mutvar` before the final `println!` is reached. In other words, the scope changes; therefore, when `mutvar` is hit on the `println!`, no borrowing is occurring and we're just displaying whatever is bound to the `mutvar` variable.

If we want to remove the braces, we will have to ensure that the borrowing has finished before we output through `println!`

It's all for your own good

These compiler rules are there to help you as a developer. They prevent the sorts of issues commonly found in other languages, the biggest being writing to a variable after it is destroyed or doing something stupid, such as trying to mutate a vector inside of a loop iterating through that vector:

```
fn main()
{
    let mut myvec = vec![5i32, 10i32, 15i32, 20i32, 25i32, 30i32];
    for i in &myvec
    {
        println!("i = {}", i);
        myvec.push(35i32);
    }
}
```

The source for this section is in the `08/invaliditerator` folder in the supporting code bundle for this book, with additional discussion in Chapter 5, *Memory Management*.

This is obviously never going to work. If you think about it, we have a loop that takes `myvec` as the argument and then, within the loop, we will add to the vector, so the loop never knows about one of the guarantees, as that guarantee is not there: the iterator count. It won't build as well because we are breaking the second borrowing rule.

The lifetime

Let's consider another piece of code which won't work:

```
let varname: &f32;
{
    let x = 3.14f32;
    varname = &x;
}
println!("varname = {}", varname);
```

When trying to build this piece of code, the compiler will complain as follows:

```
                    invalidlifetime — -bash — 80×28
Pauls-MacBook-Pro:invalidlifetime PFJ$ cargo run
    Compiling invalidlifetime v0.1.0 (file:///Users/PFJ/Dropbox/Rust/Chapter%208%
20-%20Lifecycle/Code/invalidlifetime)
src/main.rs:6:20: 6:21 error: `x` does not live long enough
src/main.rs:6          varname = &x;
                               ^
src/main.rs:3:24: 9:2 note: reference must be valid for the block suffix followi
ng statement 0 at 3:23...
src/main.rs:3    let varname : &f32;
src/main.rs:4    {
src/main.rs:5        let x = 3.14f32;
src/main.rs:6        varname = &x;
src/main.rs:7    }
src/main.rs:8    println!("varname = {}", varname);
                 ...
src/main.rs:5:25: 7:6 note: ...but borrowed value is only valid for the block su
ffix following statement 0 at 5:24
src/main.rs:5        let x = 3.14f32;
src/main.rs:6        varname = &x;
src/main.rs:7    }
error: aborting due to previous error
Could not compile `invalidlifetime`.
```

You may recall that we had something similar to the following piece of code back in Chapter 4, *Conditions, Recursion, and Loops*:

```
let y: &f32;
{
    let x_squared = x * x;
    let x_cube = x_squared * x;
    y = &(x_cube + x_squared + x);
};
println!("Y = {}", *y);
```

In Chapter 5, *Memory Management*, we then explained why the preceding code would not work.

We are assigning y to the value of a variable that only exists in a small scope and then trying to access that value, which is giving rise to undefined behavior. As we've seen, the Rust compiler will do everything it can to prevent this sort of error. In this case, the compiler keeps track of each and every reference and fails to build if a reference lasts longer than the pointer in use.

We have the same happening here: `varname` is declared before x; therefore, it lives longer than x, which is what gives rise to the error.

The preceding code is a simple demonstration of a lifetime, but it's not as simple as that.

The mythical bank account

To demonstrate a more complex problem with lifetimes, let's consider a mythical bank account:

- I am given access to a bank account, legally, of course
- I decide that I want my friend to have access to it
- After a certain amount of time, I decide I no longer want access to the account and have my access removed
- My friend then tries to use the account

When my friend comes to use the account, he is unable to do so, as the reference I had, and which was passed to him, no longer exists. He is trying to *use after free* (in programming terms) and he is known here as a **dangling reference**.

It sounds far-fetched, but in development terms, it happens far more frequently than you would possibly give credit for.

The lifetime variable - '

We have two types of lifetime within Rust—implicit and explicit. We have seen the implicit functions plenty of times:

```
fn myfunction(pi: &f32)
{
    // do something
}
```

The lifetime of the function is the length of time the code inside of the braces exists once it is called.

We also have an explicit lifetime, denoted by ' before the name:

```
fn expfunction<'a>(pi: &'a f32)
{
    // do something
}
```

However, what exactly does the 'a mean?

It means, for the lifetime of a. The <> after expfunction means that the function is taking a generic parameter (these will all become clear in Chapter 9, *Generics and Traits*), but it means of a type. If you consider Vec, it is actually Vec<T>. When we create a vector of type f32, T becomes f32, so it's Vec<f32> when it comes to compile time. In the case of expfunction, T is 'a, and therefore the type inside the () has to also be 'a.

If we had another parameter within the <>, we would have <'a, 'b>(f: &'a f32, g: &'b i32), and so on.

Lifetime of other types

We will commonly see lifetimes expressed with the likes of struct and impl (impl and the impl lifetime are dealt with in Chapter 10, *Matching and Structures*). You can have multiple lifetimes used as well.

Lifetime within an struct

As seen in Chapter 7, *Structs,* within Rust have a special purpose and they can also take multiple types within them and can be extended as much as required with as many parameters as required. Let's consider the following piece of code as an example:

```
struct MyStruct
{
    a: i32,
    b: f32,
    c: bool,
}
```

The preceding code creates a `struct` called `MyStruct` with three properties called `a`, `b`, and `c`. When an instance of `mystruct` is called into scope, the elements within `struct` can be readily accessed. If we want `struct` to be able to take a lifetime variable, we will have to both explicitly ask `struct` to take that lifetime variable and then allocate it to an element, as shown in the following code:

```
struct<'a> MyStruct
{
    lifetimevar: &'a f32,
    nvar: i32,
}
```

With the lifetime variable in there, we can be assured that the structure cannot outlive the `f32` reference it was passed to.

Multiple lifetimes

Both of these are acceptable to define multiple lifetimes within a function:

```
fn mylifetime<'a>(life: &'a i32, universe: &'a i32) -> &'a i32
{
    // do something, return an i32 value
}
```

We have two parameters of the lifetime of 'a cast as an i32 value and return an i32 value.

We can also have multiple lifetimes passed in, as follows:

```
fn mymultilife<'a, 'b>(foo: &'a f32, bar: &'b i32)
{
    // do something
}
```

Always consider the scope

As with borrowing, we have to consider the scope to ensure that things work correctly.

The following piece of code, for example, won't work:

```
struct MyStruct<'a> {
    lifea: &'a i32,
}

fn main()
{
    let x;
    {
        let y = &5; // means let y = 5; let y = &y;
        let f = MyStruct { lifea: y };
        x = &f.lifea
    }
    println!("{}", x);
}
```

 The code for this section is in the 08/lifetimescope folder of the supporting code bundle provided along with this book.

It may not seem obvious at first why this should not work. In terms of scope, f is created after y, so is in the scope of y and y is created within the scope of x. Or is it?

When the code is built, we will get the following output:

```
                          lifetimescope — -bash — 80×43
Pauls-MacBook-Pro:lifetimescope PFJ$ cargo run
   Compiling lifetimescope v0.1.0 (file:///Users/PFJ/Dropbox/Rust/Chapter%208%20
-%20Lifecycle/Code/lifetimescope)
src/main.rs:9:18: 9:19 error: borrowed value does not live long enough
src/main.rs:9          let y = &5; // means let y = 5; let y = &y;
                          ^
src/main.rs:7:11: 14:2         reference must be valid for the block suffix follow
ing statement 0 at 7:10...
src/main.rs: 7      let x;
src/main.rs: 8      {
src/main.rs: 9          let y = &5; // means let y = 5; let y = &y;
src/main.rs:10          let f = mystruct { lifea: y };
src/main.rs:11          x = &f.lifea
src/main.rs:12      }
                ...
src/main.rs:9:20: 12:6         ...but borrowed value is only valid for the block s
uffix following statement 0 at 9:19
src/main.rs: 9          let y = &5; // means let y = 5; let y = &y;
src/main.rs:10          let f = mystruct { lifea: y };
src/main.rs:11          x = &f.lifea
src/main.rs:12      }
src/main.rs:11:14: 11:21 error: `f.lifea` does not live long enough
src/main.rs:11          x = &f.lifea
                           ^~~~~~~~
src/main.rs:7:11: 14:2         reference must be valid for the block suffix follow
ing statement 0 at 7:10...
src/main.rs: 7      let x;
src/main.rs: 8      {
src/main.rs: 9          let y = &5; // means let y = 5; let y = &y;
src/main.rs:10          let f = mystruct { lifea: y };
src/main.rs:11          x = &f.lifea
src/main.rs:12      }
                ...
src/main.rs:10:39: 12:6        ...but borrowed value is only valid for the block
suffix following statement 1 at 10:38
src/main.rs:10          let f = mystruct { lifea: y };
src/main.rs:11          x = &f.lifea
src/main.rs:12      }
error: aborting due to 2 previous errors
Could not compile `lifetimescope`.

To learn more, run the command again with --verbose.
Pauls-MacBook-Pro:lifetimescope PFJ$ []
```

The error will be the x = &f.lifea, as we attempted to assign a value of something about to go out of scope.

'struct

One aspect of many languages that is useful is to have a variable that lives for the lifetime of the entire application. While some purists argue that having a variable that lasts for the life of an application is not good practice, they cannot argue that it has its uses.

Within Rust, we can also do this using a special `struct` type, a lifetime `struct`:

```
let version: &'static str = "v1.3, 22nd May 2016";
```

Local type inference allows us to omit the type when it is not global, so this is equivalent to the above when inside a function:

```
let version = "v1.3, 22nd May 2016";
```

Input and output lifetimes

Although not commonly considered, there are two types of lifetimes: input (going into the function) and output (coming out of the function).

Input only

The following code snippet is an example of a function with an input lifetime:

```
fn inponlyfn<'a>(inp: &'a as i32) {...}
```

Output only

The following code snippet is an example of a function with an output lifetime:

```
fn outonlyfn<'a>() -> &'a as i32 {...}
```

Input and output

The following code snippet is an example of a function with both input and output lifetimes:

```
fn inandout<'a>(inp: &'a str) -> &'a str {...}
```

We can conclude the following from the preceding code snippet:

- Each lifetime in the function argument becomes a distinct lifetime parameter
- If there is one input lifetime, the lifetime is assigned to all lifetimes in the return value

There is another concept that we will need to include: if there are multiple input lifetimes and one of them points to `&self` (either mutable or immutable), the lifetime of self applies to all output lifetimes.

Summary

Understanding how Rust deals with the lifetime of variables is of key importance in ensuring that as few mistakes as possible are made when creating your Rust applications. We have considered how information is moved around functions and seen how the Rust model ensures that we are never left with dangling references or code that is addressing a memory location that no longer belongs to the variable. We have also seen how Rust removes the ability to have data-race conditions.

In the next chapter, we will consider generic types, their importance to your Rust application, and how the compiler deals with them.

9

Introducing Generics, Impl, and Traits

One of the key benefits of any modern language is the ability to be able to use a type which can be anything. Not only does this reduce the amount of code required, but it allows for greater flexibility in code creation. Rust not only allows for generic types and functions, but introduces traits; these can be considered as a logical extension of generics, as they tell the compiler the functionality the type must provide.

In this chapter, we will take a look at the following topics:

- Generics in Rust
- Impl and traits
- Generic types
- Trait objects

Generics 101

For those coming from the likes of C++ and C#, generics will be nothing new to you. It is typically represented as T. It is used in the same way as a standard type. As T doesn't actually have a type, it's known a **polymorphic parameter**.

There's a simple rule regarding generic types.

The types have to match—if we define T as being f64 and attempt to assign a String to it, the compiler will fail to build that code.

While T is also (probably) the most commonly used letter for a generic type, in reality you can have any letter, or even words.

For example, this is perfectly acceptable code:

```
enum Result<Y, N>
{
    Ok(Y),
    Err(N),
}
```

Y and N do not need to be the same type either; therefore, Y could be a String and N a bool.

In practice, the following shows how the generic type works. Option is provided as part of the standard library:

```
enum Option<T>
{
    Some_Type(T),
    None
}
let varname: Option<f32> = Some_Type(3.1416f32);
```

Generics also provide another useful facility: they allow for the production of generic functions.

Generic functions—the functions that you can throw anything at! A standard function may look like this:

```
fn defined_type_fn(x: i32)
{
    // do something with x
}
```

The example code for this section can be found in 09/multiply_generic_return_t.

The parameter being passed in is an i32 and is called x. If we attempt to pass in a float, bool, string, or any other type that is not an i32, the compiler will fail the build as the types don't match.

The generic function looks very similar:

```
fn generic_type_fn<T>(x: T)
{
    // do something with x
}
```

In style, this is very similar to how a generic method is written in C#:

```
void generic_type_method<T>(T x)
{
    // do something
}
```

This can be extended to take multiple parameters with the same type:

```
fn generic_type_fn<T>(x: T, y: T)
{
    // do something
}
```

Or with multiple types and parameters:

```
fn generic_types_fn<T, U, V>(x: T, y: U, z: V)
{
    // do something
}
```

Finally, we can use a generic as a return type. Recall that a standard function returns a value like this:

```
fn multiply(a: i32, b: i32) -> i32
{
    return a * b;
}
```

The generic return would be as follows:

```
fn multiply_generic<T>(a: T, b: T) -> T
{
    return a * b;
}
```

This will only work for simplesome types; you cannot multiply string types, though you can concatenate them—this means you add one string to another. The problem though is we cannot do this... yet.

When we attempt to build this, an error is generated:

```
Binary operation '*' cannot be applied to type 'T'; an implementation of
'std::ops::Mul' might be missing for 'T'
```

Let's see if we can break this down a bit to see why we're getting the error.

Understanding the error

We know that both a and b are of type T, but what is the *real* type of a?

Here, a needs to be any type that implements std::ops::Mul—that is, the * operator. Moreover, the output of this function needs to be explicitly filled in also.

 When you see something akin to std::ops::Mul, it is just saying we're going to use the equivalent of namespace std.ops (if we are using C#). It's just the library in use.

Let's alter the type to tell the compiler that T needs to implement Mul and that we are going yield a result of type T:

```
fn multiply_generic<T: Mul<Output = T>>(a: T, b: T) -> T
{
    return a * b;
}
```

All <T: Mul<Output = T>> means is that we're going to use Mul and that the output is going to be of type T.

This time, we can build and the code works fine, as shown in the following screenshot:

```
                    generic_multiply_return_t — -bash — 80×24
Pauls-iMac:generic_multiply_return_t PFJ$ cargo build
    Compiling generic_multiply_return_t v0.1.0 (file:///Users/PFJ/Dropbox/Rust/Ch
apter%208%20-%20Generics/Code/generic_multiply_return_t)
Pauls-iMac:generic_multiply_return_t PFJ$ cargo run
     Running `target/debug/generic_multiply_return_t`
3 * 3 = 9
3.14 * 3.14 = 9.859601
Pauls-iMac:generic_multiply_return_t PFJ$ 
```

Pretty handy! By the way, there's another way to declare this:

```
fn multiply_generic<T>(a: T, b: T) -> T
  where T: Mul<Output = T>
{
  return a * b;
}
```

Whichever is neater is up to the programmer, so you may see and use both styles.

The question is: What happens if we do something like send in a string? Thankfully, in this form, the compiler throws an error and won't allow the code to build:

```
                    generic_multiply_return_t — -bash — 80×30
Pauls-iMac:generic_multiply_return_t PFJ$ cargo run
   Compiling generic_multiply_return_t v0.1.0 (file:///Users/PFJ/Dropbox/Rust/Ch
apter%208%20-%20Generics/Code/generic_multiply_return_t)
src/main.rs:12:33: 12:49 error: the trait `core::ops::Mul` is not implemented fo
r the type `&str` [E0277]
src/main.rs:12    println!("heb * ollie = {}", multiple_generic("heb", "ollie"))
;
                                              ^~~~~~~~~~~~~~~~~~~
         in expansion of format_args!
<std macros>:2:25: 2:56       expansion site
<std macros>:1:1: 2:62        in expansion of print!
<std macros>:3:1: 3:54        expansion site
<std macros>:1:1: 3:58        in expansion of println!
src/main.rs:12:4: 12:67       expansion site
src/main.rs:12:33: 12:49 error: the trait `core::ops::Mul` is not implemented fo
r the type `&str` [E0277]
src/main.rs:12    println!("heb * ollie = {}", multiple_generic("heb", "ollie"))
;
                                              ^~~~~~~~~~~~~~~~~~~
         in expansion of format_args!
<std macros>:2:25: 2:56       expansion site
<std macros>:1:1: 2:62        in expansion of print!
<std macros>:3:1: 3:54        expansion site
<std macros>:1:1: 3:58        in expansion of println!
src/main.rs:12:4: 12:67       expansion site
error: aborting due to 2 previous errors
Could not compile `generic_multiply_return_t`.

To learn more, run the command again with --verbose.
Pauls-iMac:generic_multiply_return_t PFJ$
```

A generic problem

An aspect of generics is the determination of what `T` is and therefore how we can handle it. In C#, we can use `System.Reflection` and use the `GetType` method to find the type or use `typeof` when comparing types.

 The source code for this part can be found in `09/generic_typeof`.

In Rust, we use `std::any:Any`. This is a type to emulate dynamic typing:

```
Pauls-iMac:generic_typeof PFJ$ cargo run
   Compiling generic_typeof v0.1.0 (file:///Users/PFJ/Dropbox/Rust/Chapter%208%2
0-%20Generics/Code/generic_typeof)
    Running `target/debug/generic_typeof`
TypeId { t: 10549903070749400615 }
TypeId { t: 10645063183773766558 }
TypeId { t: 17162490774200000607 }
Pauls-iMac:generic_typeof PFJ$ 
```

Just by looking at this output, you may be thinking: *What on earth are those numbers? I expected something like f32.*

 The associated code for this part can be found in `09/generic_typeof_print`.

What we're seeing here is the *ID* for the type rather than the type. To actually show the variable type, we have do something slightly different:

```
#![feature(core_intrinsics)]
fn display_type<T>(_: &T)
{
  let typename = unsafe {std::intrinsics::type_name::<T>()};
  println!("{}", typename);
}

fn main()
```

```
{
  display_type(&3.14f32);
  display_type(&1i32);
  display_type(&1.555);
  display_type(&(vec!(1,3,5)));
}
```

 At the time of writing, this code will only build on the nightly branch. Chances are that by the time you read this book, it will be in the stable branch.

When the preceding code is run on the Rust Playground website, the following results are obtained:

```
f32
i32
f64
std::vec::Vec<i32>

Program ended.
```

While most of the code we have seen many times, we have not yet come across `unsafe` and the shebang (#!) in the code.

The unsafe directive

We have seen many times so far the lengths to which the Rust compiler will go to ensure the code you have written will not only compile, but is also not going to do something stupid (such as exceed the bounds of an array, use the wrong type, or plain use a variable that has not been given a value first).

This is known as *safe* code. That's not to say that all safe code is good code—you can still end up with memory leaks, integer overflows, or threading deadlocks which you don't want, but aren't actually defined as unsafe.

In Rust, `unsafe` surrounding code means exactly that—you're telling the compiler that you know what you're writing is to be ignored by the inbuilt protection.

Using `unsafe` should only be done with care. We will come across `unsafe` later.

The whole #!

For those used to Linux shell scripting, you will have certainly seen #!—in Rust, the # is a declaration with the name in [] an attribute. They can be written as either #[attr] or #![attr].

However, the meaning of #[attr] and #![attr] is different. #[attr] only applies directly to what comes after it. The #! changes what the attribute is applied to.

We have seen this back in Chapter 2, *Variables and Variable Types*, when we discussed writing tests. We would have something like this:

```
#[test]
fn do_check()
{
  // perform check
}
```

This do_check function will only be run when we're running the tests.

Traits and Impl

A very powerful feature of Rust that is commonly seen when dealing with generics is that it is possible to tell the compiler that a particular type will provide certain functionality. This is provided by a special feature known as a trait.

However, to appreciate traits, we first have to look at the impl keyword (short for implement).

Impl

The impl keyword works in a very similar way to a function. The structure of an implementation needs to considered as being closer to a static class (in C#) or as a function within a function:

```
impl MyImpl
{
  fn reference_name (&self) ...
}
```

This would be more for a non-generic type. For generics, the preceding code becomes the following:

```
impl <T> MyGenericImpl<T>
{
   fn reference_name(&self) ...
}
```

Note that the `<T>` is required to tell the compiler that the `impl` is for a generic. `reference_name` is the name used to access the `impl` function. It can be anything you wish.

An example of `impl` can be found in `09/impl_example`.

If you build and run the `impl_example` code, you will get a result like this:

```
Pauls-iMac:impl_example PFJ$ cargo run
   Compiling impl_example v0.1.0 (file:///Users/PFJ/Dropbox/Rust/Chapter%208%20-
%20Generics/Code/impl_example)
     Running 'target/debug/impl_example'
x = 3.1415, y = 3
Pauls-iMac:impl_example PFJ$
```

The code creates two implementations for two functions that provide a defined functionality.

The `impl_example` is a very simple example. An `impl` can be as complex as required.

The impl lifetime

As mentioned in Chapter 8, *The Rust Application Lifetime*, we can use a lifetime with an `impl`:

```
impl<'a> MyFunction<'a>(varname: &'a as i32) {...}
```

`'a` is denoted directly after both the `impl` and `MyFunction`. For the `impl`, it's to say we're using it, while after `MyFunction`, it's to say we're using it within `MyFunction`.

And back to traits we go...

The simplest way to think of a trait is that it creates a signature to the implementation. If you're used to C (or C++), then you will have seen this in code akin to this:

```c
// mylib.h
int myFunction(int a, int b, float c);

// mylib.c
#include "mylib.h"
int myFunction(int a, int b, float c)
{
  // implement the code
  return some_value;
}

// myotherfile.c
#include "mylib.h"
int some_function()
{
  int value = myFunction(1, 2, 3.14f);
  return value;
}
```

The compiler accepts this code is correct as there is a signature in the .h file that says somewhere there is a compiled function that provides the implementation of this call. When the compiler comes to link everything together, the code that was promised by the signature is found and myFunction does whatever it's supposed to do and returns the int.

In C#, this would be supplied via an interface.

With Rust, we have something very similar.

The trait supplies the signature, the impl supplies the implementation, and the code calls the impl.

Now this may seem somewhat like overkill. Why would you create a stub when the implementation is typically in the same source file? The answer is we can use traits in a Rust library known as a **crate**. The trait tells the compiler that somewhere the code is implemented and it will be linked at the last stage of the build.

We will look at crates in the next chapter.

A simple crate example

In this example, we will create a trait that will contain the signature for two functions: `calc_perimeter` and `calc_area`. To start with, we construct a `struct`. In this case, we will have two `struct`s:

```
struct Perimeter
{
    side_one: i32,
    side_two: i32,
}

struct Oval
{
    radius: f32,
    height: f32,
}
```

We need to create a trait for each. The general format for a trait looks like this:

```
trait TraitName
{
    fn function_name(&self) -> return_type;
}
```

In our case, we would have the following:

```
trait CalcPerimeter
{
    fn calc_perimeter(&self) -> i32;
}

trait CalcArea
{
    fn calc_area(&self) -> f32;
}
```

We now need to create an implementation for both of these traits. The `impl`, though, will not look quite the same.

Before, we had the following:

```
impl SomeImplement
{
    ...
}
```

This time, we have to give the name of the struct it relates to:

```
impl SomeImplement for MyStruct
{
  ...
}
```

If the `impl` defines the trait and the trait is just a stub, why do we need to say which struct it is for?

This is a fair question.

Without the trait, an `impl` operates in a similar way to a function. We supply the parameters to the `impl` via `&self`. When we have a trait, the `impl` has to say what `&self` refers to.

 The code for this can be found in `09/non_generic_trait`.

Our `impl` for the first trait will be as follows:

```
impl CalcPerimeter for Perimeter
{
  fn calc_perimeter(&self) -> i32
  {
    self.side_one * 2 + self.side_two * 2
  }
}
```

Note that the function can access `side_one` and `side_two` from the `Perimeter struct`.

The second `impl` will look like this:

```
impl CalcArea for Oval
{
  fn calc_area(&self) -> f32
  {
    3.1415927f32 * self.radius * self.height
  }
}
```

Finally, the calls to the implementations. Unlike previous examples, both of the structures have to be initialized and then the implementation call given:

```
fn main()
{
  let peri = Perimeter
  {
    side_one: 5, side_two: 12 };
    println!("Side 1 = 5, Side 2 = 12, Perimeter = {}",
            peri.calc_perimeter());
    let area = Oval
    {
      radius: 5.1f32,
      height: 12.3f32
    };
    println!("Radius = 5.1, Height = 12.3, Area = {}",
            area.calc_area()); }
```

Once the code has been compiled, the expected answer is as shown in the following screenshot:

```
                    non_generic_trait — -bash — 80×24
Pauls-MacBook-Pro:non_generic_trait PFJ$ cargo run
     Running `target/debug/non_generic_trait`
Side 1 = 5, Side 2 = 12, Perimeter = 34
Radius = 5.1, Height = 12.3, Area = 197.07211
Pauls-MacBook-Pro:non_generic_trait PFJ$
```

Traits and generics

If we look at the code, we have two structures that effectively do the same thing, with the only difference being the types for the parameters aren't the same. We can alter the member names for the structures without an issue to make life simpler:

```
struct Perimeter { side_one: i32, side_two: i32, }
struct Oval { radius: f32, height: f32, }
```

This would become the following:

```
struct Shape<T> { line_one: T, line_two: T, }
```

The calculation cannot be altered as they are totally different, but will need the parameter names to be altered. The other aspect to alter will be the name for the functions. Let's create a version of the code that only uses part of the code.

As we have the generic version of the `struct`, we next need to create the trait:

```
trait Calculate<T> { fn calc(&self) -> T; }
```

We have to use `<T>` as the `trait` has to take a generic.

The construction for the implementation can be achieved in one of two ways.

 The code for this section can be found in `09/generic_traits_simple`.

Defining the impl for specific types

This is by far the simplest way of creating the code. We define the types that `Shape` can take:

```
impl Calculate<i32> for Shape<i32>
{
  fn calc(&self) -> i32
  {
    self.line_one * 2 + self.line_two * 2
  }
}
```

Writing the code like this ensures that we cannot pass anything into the implementations that don't make any sense (for example, types that cannot have + or * applied to them).

Using where

If you're used to programming using generics in C#, this should be familiar to you.

Rust contains an implementation of `where`, so we are able to define what `where` is. This means that, as we had in an earlier example for this chapter, the construct `<T : Mul<Output = T>>` can be used in a modified way:

```
impl<T> Calculate<T> for Shape<T> where T: Mul<Output = T>
```

This does, though, give rise to a number of other issues. Two simple ones are that we multiply by 2—however, that value isn't clear if it's 2u8 or 2i32. We also try to add values together, but as with multiplying T together, there is no guarantee you can add by T.

Making it work

The final step is to add a main function. We can use the same function as was in the non-generic trait example but with the oval removed:

```
fn main()
{
  let peri = Shape
  {
    line_one: 5,
    line_two: 12
  };
  println!("line_one = 5, line_two = 12, Perimeter = {}",
           peri.calc ());
}
```

When compiled, this gives the following output:

```
                        generic_traits_simple — -bash — 80×30
Pauls-iMac:generic_traits_simple PFJ$ cargo run
    Compiling generic_traits_simple v0.1.0 (file:///Users/PFJ/Dropbox/Rust/Chapte
r%208%20-%20Generics/Code/generic_traits_simple)
      Running `target/debug/generic_traits_simple`
line_one = 5, line_two = 12, perimeter = 34
Pauls-iMac:generic_traits_simple PFJ$ 
```

As we have created the second implementation, extending the main function to include the second calculation should be trivial.

See 09/generic_trait_full for the code files of this part.

We also need to implement the `f32` calculation:

```
impl Calculate<f32> for Shape<f32>
{
  fn calc(&self) -> f32
  {
    3.1415927f32 * self.line_one * self.line_two
  }
}
```

When this is compiled, we see the following:

```
                      generic_trait_full — -bash — 80×30
Pauls-iMac:generic_trait_full PFJ$ cargo run
    Compiling generic_trait_full v0.1.0 (file:///Users/PFJ/Dropbox/Rust/Chapter%2
08%20-%20Generics/Code/generic_trait_full)
     Running `target/debug/generic_trait_full`
line_one = 5, line_two = 12, perimeter = 34
line_one = 5.1f32, line_two = 12.3f32, area = 197.07211
Pauls-iMac:generic_trait_full PFJ$ 
```

Something you may have noticed

If we compare the two different implementations of the code (generic and non-generic), the main difference is that we have reduced the amount of code we need as the two structs were the same in all but the name. We have also simplified the code so that we have a single call to calc and allow the compiler to decide which one we need based on the type passed in.

Generics - a small aside

Code reduction and simplification is always a good thing (well, mostly at least!). However, with generics, there is always a trade-off and it's not always apparent.

Let's consider the following piece of code:

```
fn my_multiply<T: Mul<Output = T>>(a: T, b: T) -> T { return a * b; }
```

This returns a value of type T by multiplying two variables (of type T).

The question is: You can send a number of types into that function - how will the compiler know what to do if it doesn't know what type T is? The only safe way is to create a version of `my_multiply` for each possible type. Fortunately, the compiler does this automatically for you in a process called monomorphization.

So what does happen?

To give all of these generated functions unique names, compilers that work with generics use a process called **name mangling** (or *name munging*). This creates a unique name for each internally created function that takes generic parameters.

For which one to use, during linking, the linker analyzes the code *signatures* required. If the linker sees a signature requiring `f32` for T, that munged name object code is included in the final object list. Once the linker has finished with the analysis, the unused objects (those not on the final list) are stripped out. The final binary therefore only contains the required code and not every variation of the types possible.

> While different compilers treat generics differently, the process for compilation, name munging, and then final stripping is common among them all!

Back to the where version

The `where` version of the code is more complex than the non-where version.

> The source for this version can be found in `09/generic_trait_where`.

Let's examine the code:

```
extern crate num;
use std::ops::{Add, Mul};
use num::FromPrimitive;
```

We have seen `std::ops::Mul` before in the generic multiplication example. If we need to include multiple items from `std::ops` (or indeed any library), they are held in curly braces; `{}`. Here, we include `Add` and `Mul`.

Up until this point, we have not seen the `extern crate` directive. For now, it is enough to know that this will include an external library. Crates are covered in Chapter 9, *Generics and Traits*.

Finally, we use `FromPrimitive` from the `num` library.

Our `struct` and `trait` are the same as before. The implementation, though, is different:

```
impl<T> Calculate<T> for Shape<T>
  where T: Copy + FromPrimitive + Add<Output = T> +
  Mul<Output = T>
{
  fn calc(&self) -> T {
    let two = T::from_u8(2).expect("Unable to create a value of 2");
    self.line_one * two + self.line_two * two
  }
}
```

There are two important lines in this code: `where T:Copy + FromPrimitive + Add<Output = T> + Mul<Output = T>` and `let two = T::from_u8(2).expect("Unable to create a value of 2");`.

Here, we are saying that we want to copy the type, we'll be using `FromPrimitive` to cast a primitive to `T`, and both the `Add` and `Mul` outputs will be of type `T`. Rust concatenates the parameters that a `where` uses using `+`.

The `let two` line creates a variable that takes an unsigned 8-bit value and casts that to `T`. If it fails, the error is thrown.

We have to use `Add<Output = T>` to ensure we can add the types together.

Try to compile

If you use the standard `cargo run`, you will be met with an error that the compiler is unable to find `extern crate num`. This is down to cargo not knowing where the dependencies are held. At the first time of grabbing an external reference, Rust will update the list of available crates (the registry) and then download the ones required. To do this, the `Cargo.toml` file needs to be edited and the following code inserted:

```
[dependencies]
num = "*"
```

Once this has been saved and the `cargo run` executed, you will see output like this:

```
Pauls-iMac:generic_trait_where PFJ$ cargo run
    Updating registry `https://github.com/rust-lang/crates.io-index`
 Downloading num-bigint v0.1.32
 Downloading num-rational v0.1.32
 Downloading num-iter v0.1.32
 Downloading num-complex v0.1.32
 Downloading num-integer v0.1.32
 Downloading rustc-serialize v0.3.19
 Downloading num v0.1.32
 Downloading num-traits v0.1.32
 Downloading rand v0.3.14
 Downloading libc v0.2.10
   Compiling libc v0.2.10
   Compiling rustc-serialize v0.3.19
   Compiling num-traits v0.1.32
   Compiling rand v0.3.14
   Compiling num-integer v0.1.32
   Compiling num-complex v0.1.32
   Compiling num-iter v0.1.32
   Compiling num-bigint v0.1.32
   Compiling num-rational v0.1.32
   Compiling num v0.1.32
   Compiling generic_trait_where v0.1.0 (file:///Users/PFJ/Dropbox/Rust/Chapter%
208%20-%20Generics/Code/generic_trait_where)
     Running `target/debug/generic_trait_where`
line_one = 5, line_two = 12, perimeter = 34
```

Trait bounds

A trait can also have a bound placed upon it. In effect, a bound is a rule that the trait has to abide by and is added to the declaring type parameter.

 The source for this part is in `09/trait_bound_gen_struct`.

In the code example, the `impl` has a `PartialEq` bound placed upon the generic type. Our `struct` contains four parameters within it and so we only want to test for partial equality within that `struct`. If we didn't have the `PartialEq` on the declared type parameter, the compilation would fail as we're not testing everything within that `struct`.

When the code is compiled, we get the following output:

```
Pauls-iMac:trait_bound_gen_struct PFJ$ cargo run
     Running `target/debug/trait_bound_gen_struct`
test_one != test_two
test_one == test_two
Pauls-iMac:trait_bound_gen_struct PFJ$ 
```

Can we reduce the amount of code further?

Yes. It is possible to completely omit the requirement to create an implementation of a trait if that trait contains a default method:

```
trait MyTrait
{
    fn test_code(&self) -> bool;
    fn self_test_code(&self) -> bool { self.test_code() } }
```

`test_code` is just the stub which requires an implementation. The `self_test_code` function doesn't need an implementation as it has a default method already.

Can the default method be overridden?

It can.

The code for this section is in `09/override_default_method`.

Let's start the code off by defining a `trait`. This has a default method for `is_not_done`. We will still need to implement `is_done` though, which we do for the `UseFirstTime` struct:

```
struct UseFirstTime;
impl MyTrait for UseFirstTime
{
  fn is_done(&self) -> bool
  {
    println!("UseFirstTime.is_done");
    true
  }
}
```

We next want to override the default method for `is_not_done`. Again, we create an empty `struct` and write both the implementations for `is_done` and `is_not_done`. When we call `is_not_done` from the second `struct`, the `println!` from the second `struct` is shown and not the first:

```
struct OverrideFirstTime;
impl MyTrait for OverrideFirstTime
{
  fn is_done(&self) -> bool
  {
    println!("OverrideFirstTime.is_done");
    true
  }
  fn is_not_done(&self) -> bool
  {
    println!("OverrideFirstTime.is_not_done");
    true
  }
}
```

When compiled, we get the following output:

```
Pauls-iMac:override_default_method PFJ$ cargo run
    Compiling override_default_method v0.1.0 (file:///Users/PFJ/Dropbox/Rust/Chap
ter%208%20-%20Generics/Code/override_default_method)
      Running `target/debug/override_default_method`
UseFirstTime.is_done
OverrideFirstTime.is_not_done
Pauls-iMac:override_default_method PFJ$
```

Rounding off traits

```
Pauls-iMac:inheritance PFJ$ cargo run
    Compiling inheritance v0.1.0 (file:///Users/PFJ/Dropbox/Rust/Chapter%208%20-%
20Generics/Code/inheritance)
      Running `target/debug/inheritance`
one
onetwo
Pauls-iMac:inheritance PFJ$
```

This has been a large topic, but we have two more aspects to consider for traits: inheritance and deriving. One that should be familiar if you're used to any form of object-oriented programming.

Inheritance

This is very similar to inheritance within C++ and C#:

```
trait One
{
  fn one(&self);
}
trait OneTwo : One
{
  fn onetwo(&self);
}
```

Code for this part is in `09/inheritance`.

The code that implements `OneTwo` must also implement `One` (the same as when we overrode the default method, we still had to define `is_done`), therefore:

```
struct Three;
impl One for Three
{
  fn one(&self)
  {
    println!("one");
  }
}
impl OneTwo for Three
{
  fn onetwo(&self)
  {
    println!("onetwo");
  }
}
```

And the result is as follows:

```
                      inheritance — -bash — 80×30
Pauls-iMac:inheritance PFJ$ cargo run
    Compiling inheritance v0.1.0 (file:///Users/PFJ/Dropbox/Rust/Chapter%208%20-%
20Generics/Code/inheritance)
     Running `target/debug/inheritance`
one
onetwo
Pauls-iMac:inheritance PFJ$
```

If we omitted the `impl One` block, we would get a compilation error complaining that `impl OneTwo` requires `impl One` to exist.

Deriving

Rust provides a handy attribute that allows you to access a number of commonly used traits without having to implement them yourself time and again. They are called using `#[derive(Trait_Name)]`.

The traits available are as follows:

- `Clone`: This creates a clone of the object
- `Copy`: This creates a copy of the object
- `Debug`: This provides debugging code
- `Default`: This gives a useful default value for a type
- `Eq`: `Equality`, this is similar to `PartialEq` except for all parameters within a struct
- `Hash`: This is a hashable type
- `Ord`: `Order`, these are the types that form a total order on all types
- `PartialEq`: `Partial Equality`, this only tests on a subset of the struct
- `PartialOrd`: `Partial Order`, values that can compared to create a sort order

Trait objects

Typically, when we call a function in Rust, we will have a line in the code similar to this:

```
call_some_method(some_value);
```

When we have a `struct` in the code which has an `impl` attached to it, we will have this:

```
let m = MyStruct {a: 3, b: 4, c: 1, d: 4}; m.call_some_method();
```

These are both fine.

If you recall, back in the `generic_trait_full` example, we had `Calc` defined and `T` could be either an `f32` or `i32`. We also talked about how the application knew what to include in the final binary. This is known as **static dispatch** (which Rust prefers).

Rust uses a system called a **dispatch**, of which there are two types: static (favored by Rust) and dynamic. Dynamic dispatch relies on something called a **trait object**.

Let's create a sample test setup

The test code is very simple. We have a trait with a function that returns a `String`. We then have a couple of implementations and a parameter bound function that will display the result from the implementations:

```
trait StaticObject
{
   fn static_method(&self) -> String;
}

impl StaticObject for u8
{
   fn static_method(&self) -> String {format!("u8 : {}, ", *self)}
}

impl StaticObject for String
{
   fn static_method(&self) -> String {format!("string : {}", *self)}
}

fn display_code<T: StaticObject>(data : T)
{
   println!("{}", data.static_method());
}

fn main()
{
   let test_one = 8u8;
   let test_two = "Some text".to_string();
   display_code(test_one);
   display_code(test_two);
}
```

   The code for this part can be found in `09/trait_object_static`.

When compiled and executed, we get the following:

```
Pauls-iMac:trait_object_static PFJ$ cargo run
    Compiling trait_object_static v0.1.0 (file:///Users/PFJ/Dropbox/Rust/Chapter%
208%20-%20Generics/Code/trait_object_static)
    Running `target/debug/trait_object_static`
u8 : 8,
string : Some text
Pauls-iMac:trait_object_static PFJ$
```

From the previous explanation, we know that the compiler will generate the various types that T can be.

Let's see dynamic dispatch

Dynamic dispatch uses trait objects. A trait object can store a value of any type that implements the trait. The actual type of the value is only known at runtime.

 The code for this section can be found in `09/dynamic_dispatch`.

Let's look at some code to explain how this works.

Previously, we had for `display_code` the following:

```
fn display_code<T: StaticObject>(data: T)
{
  println!("{}", data.static_method());
}
```

We now have this:

```
fn display_code(data : &DynamicObject)
{
  println!("{}", data.dynamic_method());
}
```

We no longer have the `T` parameter.

In the static version, `display_code` was called like this:

```
display_code(test_one);
```

For the dynamic version, we use the following:

```
display_code(&test_one as &DynamicObject);
```

The trait object has been obtained from the pointer (`&DynamicObject`) which implemented the trait by using the cast (`&test_one as &DynamicObject`). It is also acceptable to use `display_code(&test_one)`. This is known as coercion: `&test_one` has been used as an argument to a function that takes `&DynamicObject`.

The only issue with dynamic dispatch is that it can be slower, as each time the code is run, the runtime *forgets* the type of the pointer and has to create a new implementation for the different type.

Keeping your object safe

We can't use all traits to create a trait object. Take the following:

```
let my_vec = vec![1,3,5,7,9];
let dupe = &my_vec as &Clone;
```

This will not compile as `Clone` is not object-safe as `Clone` contains `Self: Sized`, which a trait cannot have.

If the trait doesn't require `Self: Sized` and all of the methods are object-safe, it is an object-safe trait. For a method to be object-safe, it must require `Self: Sized`. If the method doesn't require `Self: Sized`, it can still be object-safe if the method doesn't require any parameters and doesn't use `Self`.

Summary

Traits and generics are a key feature for development and Rust is feature-rich for these. We have seen how to create implementations, how to use generics, how to ensure that the types can be bound, and the power of traits. Hopefully, you should be appreciating now the sheer power that generics provide to the developer in terms of flexibility. Generics also allow for reducing the amount of code we (as developers) have to write by essentially removing the need to worry too much about what the generic represents.

In the next chapter, we will be looking at extending our Rust applications by the use of external libraries, known as crates.

10
Creating Your Own Crate

Most languages allow for external libraries to be created. These typically contain commonly used pieces of code that are for general use. For example, libraries for deserializing JSON are fairly common, as are math libraries. Rust is no exception. It allows for the creation of libraries (known as **crates**). These crates can be kept to yourself or distributed however you see fit. The metadata about crates is stored on a public service, at `https://crates.io/`.

In this chapter, we will cover the following topics:

- How crates are created
- How the directory structure is used
- How crates are made up of modules
- How to include your crate within your code
- How scopes are used with your modules

What exactly is a crate?

As with all languages, Rust can use external libraries that, we've established are called crates. But what are they?

If we think about a crate, we think either of something we use to hold lots of other things. Software developers like to keep their code clean and if they know what they're doing, they tend to keep their libraries fairly specialized. These specialisms within a crate are known as modules.

 A crate is a container with one or more modules within it.

Looking at modules

To show how crates are put together, we are going to create one. In this case, it will be a simple math crate.

Before we consider this, let's consider something we all know: a car. We will consider the car a crate, as everything to do with the car is held within it.

To start, let's think about the main parts of the car: the engine, fuel, interior, wheels and movement, and electrics.

There are more but, for now, we will ignore them. Let's represent this as a block diagram to make the relationship clearer:

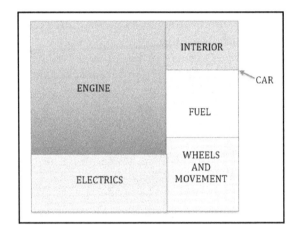

We can, of course, split up each of these blocks (for example, we can split the electrics into ignition, audio, windows, heated windscreens, lights, and interior fan).

The car is the crate. Each block is a module. Each split is a submodule. It's now quite simple to see how crates can be visualized.

I can see a problem with this analogy

There was a reason I chose a car. If we think about it, all of the parts aren't really that discrete; the engine requires fuel, the electrics are needed by the engine, but the engine also generates electricity, and so on. In terms of programming, this will lead to a horrid mess.

How can we keep them apart?

The answer is that we use a scope for each. For example, the top level for this crate would be **Car**. We then add **::** followed by the module name (**Car::Engine**, **Car::Fuel**, and so on.). If a module requires access to another module, it can be included using the usual `use` directive.

 The name of the crate is the name used when the library is created using cargo. In this example, the command line to create this crate will be as follows:
cargo new Car
Note that we do not use the `--bin` flag.

Consider the following example:

```
// in Car::Engine
use Fuel;
use Electrics;
```

If we break the modules down further, we extend the scope in the same way as we did previously in order to access them:

```
// in the main code
use Car::Interior::Audio;
use Car::Interior::Windows::HeatedRear;
```

Back to our math library

Now that we know how crates and modules go together and how their scope allows for the modules to not become confused if they function with the same name (`Car::Engine` and `Car::Electics` can both have a function called `voltage_to_earth`, for example, each does a different action), let's consider our math library.

The library will have four modules with a number of submodules:

- Trigonometry:
  - Sin/Cos/Tan
  - Arcsin, Arccos, and Arctan

- Regression analysis:
    - Intercept on a straight line
    - Standard deviation and r^2 value
- Conversions:
    - Temperature, pressure, and volume
- Base functions:
    - Base n to base 10 conversions
    - Base 10 to base n conversions
    - Base m to base n addition, subtraction, multiplication, and division

Using a useful name

Naming within a module is very important; it is going to be visible to anyone using it and should therefore describe what it does. The same applies to function names. For example, *f_to_c* is fine, but the whole point of a library is that you can get what you are after without having to second-guess what the author meant. A function name such as *fahrenheit_to_celcius* makes much more sense.

The same applies to modules. If I were to use *ra* for regression analysis, it might seem like a reasonable name to use, but is it clear? The name can mean anything here. It may seem like a lot of effort to create a module called *regression_analysis*, but it will help other users know what to expect.

Let's create!

To start, we need to create the crate itself.

To do this, instead of writing the following, we need to tell cargo that we are creating a library:

```
cargo new myapp -bin
```

To do this, we simply omit the -bin flag:

```
cargo new MathLib
```

The following screenshot shows this, followed by the tree structure for the module. You'll notice that `main.rs` has been replaced by `lib.rs`:

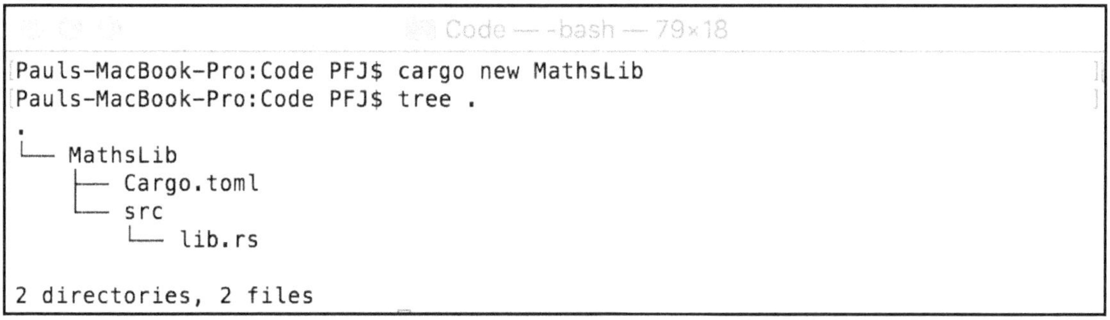

```
Code — -bash — 79×18
Pauls-MacBook-Pro:Code PFJ$ cargo new MathsLib
Pauls-MacBook-Pro:Code PFJ$ tree .
.
└── MathsLib
    ├── Cargo.toml
    └── src
        └── lib.rs

2 directories, 2 files
```

Figure 1

Creating top-level modules

To create a module, we first need to tell the compiler that the code is held in a module. In this example, I will use the `Trigonometry` module:

```
mod Trigonometry // top level module
{
    mod Natural  // sub module
    {
    }
    mod Arc      // sub module
    {
    }
}
```

When we compile this using `cargo build` (not `cargo run`; there is no `main` function within the library) and examine the tree, we'll see the library (highlighted):

```
● ● ●                          Code — -bash — 80×4
Pauls-MacBook-Pro:Code PFJ$ tree MathsLibStructure
MathsLibStructure
├── Cargo.lock
├── Cargo.toml
├── src
│   └── lib.rs
└── target
    └── debug
        ├── build
        ├── deps
        ├── examples
        ├── libMathsLibStructure.rlib
        └── native

7 directories, 4 files
```

Figure 2

The structure for this section can be found in `Chapter10/MathsLibStucture`.

We can't do very much with it currently as all it contains are placeholders that do very little. Before this goes any further, have a look at the `lib.rs` source file. With nothing in except for the module names, it hits 62 lines. Let's think of a very simple example for the `Conversion` module, *fahrenheit_to_celcius*.

The formula to do this is *(F - 32) * 5/9*. Our function will therefore be the following:

```
pub fn fahrenheit_to_celcius(a: f32) -> f32
{
    (a - 32f32) * 5f32 / 9f32
}
```

That was just four lines of code. We also need ones to go from C to F, K to C, C to K, F to K, and K to F (K is Kelvin, which denotes absolute temperature, that is, 0K = -273.15°C , also known as absolute zero). Including these will take it to a total of around 24 lines of code. This is a simple module. The ones for regression analysis run to around 100.

Our source file is going to be huge. As we want to keep our modules manageable, we are going to need to break the `lib.rs` file down a bit.

The multifile module

In order to break our current `lib.rs` file down, we are going to have to change how we declare modules.

 The source for this section is in `Chapter10/MathsLibMultiFile` and `Chapter10/MathsLibMulti FileDirs`.

Currently, we have this:

```
mod Trigonometry // top level module
{
    mod Natural  // sub module
    {
    }
    mod Arc      // sub module
    {
    }
}
```

To break this into separate files, we need to declare only the top-level modules in `lib.rs`:

```
mod Trigonometry;
mod RegressionAnalysis;
mod Conversions;
mod Bases;
```

What about submodules?

When we declare top-level modules like this, Rust will expect there to be either a directory for each of these modules or four source files (`Trigonometry.rs`, `RegressionAnalysis.rs`, `Conversions.rs`, and `Bases.rs`). If the directory structure is used, Rust will expect a file called `mod.rs` in each directory.

Let's compare how these two systems look, and then we can examine the relative benefits of each. The structure of `MathsLibMultiFile` will be as follows:

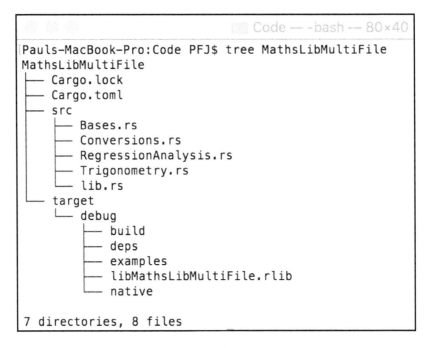

Figure 3a

The structure of `MathsLibMultiFileDirs` will be as follows:

```
                              Code — -bash — 80×40
MathsLibMultiFileDirs
├── Cargo.lock
├── Cargo.toml
├── src
│   ├── Bases
│   │   ├── BaseToBase.rs
│   │   ├── FromBase10.rs
│   │   ├── ToBase10.rs
│   │   └── mod.rs
│   ├── Conversions
│   │   ├── Distance.rs
│   │   ├── Pressure.rs
│   │   ├── Temperature.rs
│   │   ├── Volume.rs
│   │   └── mod.rs
│   ├── RegressionAnalysis
│   │   ├── Intercepts.rs
│   │   ├── Statistics.rs
│   │   └── mod.rs
│   ├── Trigonometry
│   │   ├── Arc.rs
│   │   ├── Natural.rs
│   │   └── mod.rs
│   └── lib.rs
└── target
    └── debug
        ├── build
        ├── deps
        ├── examples
        ├── libMathsLibMultiFileDirs.rlib
        └── native

11 directories, 19 files
```

Figure 3b

At first glance, they seem to be very similar; the only difference is that multifiledir (*Fig 3b*) has modules broken down into separate files whereas multifile (*Fig 3a*) only has a single file for each module. This is a limitation of the non-directory structure; the submodules are kept in a single file, which is fine for a very small module but no good for larger modules.

In the directory structure version, there is a `mod.rs` file. This is completely empty but is there to let the compiler know that we have submodules. If (say) `RegressionAnalysis::Statistics` were to be further broken down, it would be a case of creating a new directory within the `RegressionAnalysis` directory called `Statistics` (the directory must have the same name as the module) and adding a new `mod.rs` file as well as new submodules.

The mod.rs file

This file should include an interface to the module itself. The name of the module will point to a file with the same name.

Consider the following example:

```
mod mycode;
```

The preceding line will point to `mycode.rs`. You will need to include an interface to each file in that module directory (with the exception of `mod.rs`).

Let's add some code

We now have the structure in place and our basic framework; we can start adding some code to the library. In this case, it will be the `Conversions::Temperature` part. We have already seen the function for Fahrenheit to Celcius, so let's add the other functions:

```
// Temperature.rs
mod Temperature
{
    fn fahrenheit_to_celcius(f: f32) -> f32
    {
        (f - 32f32) * 5f32/9f32
    }
    fn celcius_to_fahrenheit(f: f32) -> f32
    {
        (c * (9f32/5f32)) + 32f32
    }
    fn celcius_to_kelvin(c: f32) -> f32
    {
```

```
        c + 273.15
    }
    fn kelvin_to_celcius(k: f32) -> f32
    {
        k - 273.15;
    }
    fn fahrenheit_to_kelvin(f: f32) -> f32
    {
        (f + 459.67) * 5f32 / 9f32
    }
    fn kelvin_to_fahrenheit(k: f32) -> f32
    {
        (k * (9f32 / 5f32)) - 459.67
    }
}
```

There is nothing earth-shattering about this code, but we do have to stop for a second to think about this. The Kelvin scale goes from 0 to *n*; it never goes below zero. It's entirely possible for the user to want to use `celcius_to_kelvin` and pass -274 instead. This would mean that the answer from the function would be mathematically correct but physically incorrect.

The code for this section is in `Chapter10/MathsLib`.

We could return -1 but then, for some of the functions, that answer is fine.

What we need to return here is a tuple with the first parameter being a Boolean, signifying whether the calculation is valid or not (`true` = valid). If it's `true`, the answer is in the second parameter; otherwise, pass back the original value passed in.

As a quick test, the following code can be run:

See `Chapter10/QuickTest` for the source.

```
fn kelvin_to_celcius(k: f32) -> (bool, f32)
{
    if k < 0f32
    {
        return (false, k);
    }
```

```
        else
        {
            return (true, k - 273.15);
        }
    }

    fn main()
    {
        let mut calc = kelvin_to_celcius(14.5);
        match calc.0
        {
            true => println!("14.5K = {}C", calc.1),
            _ => println!("equation was invalid"),
        }
        calc = kelvin_to_celcius(-4f32);
        match calc.0
        {
            true => println!("-4K = {}C", calc.1),
            _ => println!("invalid K"),
        }
    }
```

It is convenient here to use the indexed form of the tuple rather than destructuring it into two variables.

When compiled, we get the following output:

```
                      QuickTest — -bash — 80×40
Pauls-MacBook-Pro:Code PFJ$ cd QuickTest
Pauls-MacBook-Pro:QuickTest PFJ$ cargo run
    Compiling QuickTest v0.1.0 (file:///Users/PFJ/Dropbox/Rust/Chapter%2010%20-%2
0Crates/Code/QuickTest)
        crate `QuickTest` should have a snake case name such as `quick_test`, #
[warn(non_snake_case)] on by default
    Running `target/debug/QuickTest`
14.5K = -258.65C
invalid K
```

Figure 4

This is exactly what was expected. It does also show a need for a set of unit tests to be added into the library to determine the validity (or not) of the data being fed in.

Beware of double name scopes

It is quite a common problem to create a crate that may run into an issue known as double name scope. Consider the following example:

```
mathslib::conversions::temperature::temperature
```

Writing the preceding line instead of the following line causes a major problem:

```
mathslib::conversions::temperature;
```

The problem is down to the mod.rs and the temperature file.

If you look at `lib.rs`, it has in it the name of the module that has to marry up with the name of the directory, which, in turn, contains the `mod.rs` file. The `mod.rs` file (as we have seen) needs to contain a public interface to the module. Now, following this logic, the code in the `temperature.rs` file should also have `pub mod temperature { ... }`. It is this final `pub mod` that gives the double name scope.

To avoid this problem, just leave the `pub mod temperature` line out. As long as the filename matches the `pub mod` name in `mod.rs`, the compiler will consider that code as belonging to the named mod from `mod.rs`.

Check out the following code snippet:

```
// in mod.rs
pub mod temperature;
// all code in temperature.rs "belongs" to mod temperature
fn celcius_to_kelvin(c: f32) -> (bool, f32) { ... }
```

Adding unit tests to the library

We can create tests in one of the two ways: either by adding a `tests` directory with a `lib.rs` file or by simply adding a file with the tests for that module. As we are already using a directory structure, let's stay with that for the unit tests.

As previously discussed in `Chapter 1`, *Introducing and Installing Rust*, to add a unit test, we precede the code with the following:

```
#[test]
```

Then to build, we need to do the following:

```
cargo test
```

When we do this, though, we hit a problem. Our unit test file looks like this:

```
extern crate mathslib;
use mathsLib::conversions::temperature;

#[cfg(test)]
mod temperature_tests
{
    #[test]
    fn test_kelvin_to_celcius_pass()
    {
        let calc = kelvin_to_celcius(14.5);
        assert_eq!(calc.0, true);
    }
    #[test]
    #[should_panic(expected = "assertion failed")]
    fn test_kelvin_to_celcius_fail()
    {
        let calc = kelvin_to_celcius(-4f32);
        assert_eq!(calc.0,true);
    }
}
```

On the face of it, this should work, but it comes back with something that is somewhat perplexing:

```
Pauls-MacBook-Pro:MathsLib PFJ$ cargo test
   Compiling MathsLib v0.1.0 (file:///Users/PFJ/Dropbox/Rust/Chapter%2010%20-%20
Crates/Code/MathsLib)
tests/lib.rs:10:5: 10:39 error: unresolved import `MathsLib::Conversions::Temper
ature`. There is no `Temperature` in `MathsLib::Conversions` [E0432]
tests/lib.rs:10 use MathsLib::Conversions::Temperature;
                   ^~~~~~~~~~~~~~~~~~~~~~~~~~~~~~~~~~~~
tests/lib.rs:10:5: 10:39          run `rustc --explain E0432` to see a detailed exp
lanation
error: aborting due to previous error
Could not compile `MathsLib`.
```

Figure 5

This doesn't make sense; we know there is a module called Temperature, so why are we getting this message? The answer is that it's all down to the privacy of the module and functions.

Making something public

We saw in Chapter 7, *Matching and Structures*, how Rust, by default, sets all the functions, structs, and so on to be private. This is fine, as it prevents some of the nuts and bolts of the code from being exposed to the public interface.

This does mean, though, that we have to explicitly set the module, and all of the functions we want the user to have access to, to be pub (public). Therefore, our functions for the temperature conversion will be as follows:

```
pub mod Temperature
{
    pub fn fahrenheit_to_celcius(f: f32) -> f32
    {
        (f - 32f32) * 5f32/9f32
    }
}
```

The next time we come to run the unit tests, we should not have this issue, except for the following snag:

```
Pauls-MacBook-Pro:MathsLib PFJ$ cargo test
   Compiling MathsLib v0.1.0 (file:///Users/PFJ/Dropbox/Rust/Chapter%2010%20-%20
Crates/Code/MathsLib)
tests/lib.rs:18:20: 18:37 error: unresolved name `kelvin_to_celcius` [E0425]
tests/lib.rs:18          let calc = kelvin_to_celcius(14.5);
                                    ^~~~~~~~~~~~~~~~~~~~
```

Figure 6

We have definitely got a `pub` function in the `Temperature` module called `kelvin_to_celcius`. The issue is the following line:

```
use mathslib::conversions::temperature;
```

What this does is import only the module and none of the symbols (the functions). We can fix this in one of the following four ways:

- We can use the following:

```
use mathslib::conversions::temperature::*;
```

- We use the following:

```
use mathslib::conversions::temperature::kelvin_to_celcius;
```

- We use the following:

  `use mathslib::conversions::temperature;` then precede `kelvin_to_celcius` with `temperature::`

- We remove the `use mathslib` line and add the following line inside `mod temperature_tests`:

```
use super::*;
```

Using any of these should allow the tests to compile and run. The output you will see should be something like this:

```
Pauls-MacBook-Pro:mathslib PFJ$ cargo test
   Compiling mathslib v0.1.0 (file:///Users/PFJ/Dropbox/Rust/Chapter%2010%20-%20
Crates/Code/mathslib)
     Running target/debug/lib-0ce032ad6dfb1f5e

running 2 tests
test conversion_tests::temperature_tests::temperature_test::test_kelvin_to_celci
us_pass ... ok
test conversion_tests::temperature_tests::temperature_test::test_kelvin_to_celci
us_fail ... ok

test result: ok. 2 passed; 0 failed; 0 ignored; 0 measured

     Running target/debug/mathslib-7f789d0d747a1a78

running 0 tests

test result: ok. 0 passed; 0 failed; 0 ignored; 0 measured

   Doc-tests mathslib

running 0 tests

test result: ok. 0 passed; 0 failed; 0 ignored; 0 measured
```

Fig 7: chap10_unittest

Let's give our crate a quick run out

As it stands, our crate is far from finished. However, there is enough code in there to see whether it actually runs.

Code for this section is in Chapter10/first_run_out.

Our initial code looks like this:

```
extern crate mathslib;
use mathslib::conversions::temperature::*;
fn main()
{
    let mut testval = celcius_to_fahrenheit(100f32);
    println!("100C = {}F", testval.1); // should be 212
}
```

When we build this, we get the following:

```
                    src — -bash — 80×11
Pauls-MacBook-Pro:src PFJ$ cargo run
   Compiling first_run_out v0.1.0 (file:///Users/PFJ/Dropbox/Rust/Chapter%2010%2
0-%20Crates/Code/first_run_out)
main.rs:1:1: 1:23 error: can't find crate for `mathslib` [E0463]
main.rs:1 extern crate mathslib;
          ^~~~~~~~~~~~~~~~~~~~~~~
error: aborting due to previous error
Could not compile `first_run_out`.

To learn more, run the command again with --verbose.
Pauls-MacBook-Pro:src PFJ$ []
```

Figure 7

This stands to reason; we're asking the code to include a library that it has no clue about.

External dependencies

Normally, if a dependency is outside the application, we would add something like this to the `Cargo.toml` file:

```
[dependencies]
mathslib = "0.1.0"
```

In this case, we're not able to use cargo to make the build; instead, we need to compile using `rustc`. The way cargo works is it recompiles the dependencies for each project (there is no guarantee that each project will use the same set of features for a given crate).

We can simulate a cargo run with the following command:

```
rustc -L . src/main.rs && ./main
```

The `-L` links any libraries in `.` (the root directory, where you find `Cargo.toml`) to the sources after the `.` . The `/main` part essentially tells the command-line interpreter to execute the binary called `./main` in the root directory (the name comes from the file compiled).

Once we have executed this, we can see our application in all its glory:

```
first_run_out — -bash — 80×17
Pauls-MacBook-Pro:first_run_out PFJ$ rustc -L . src/main.rs && ./main
100C = 212F
14.5C = 287.65K
Pauls-MacBook-Pro:first_run_out PFJ$
```

Figure 8

We now know that our crate (as-is) is running as it should do.

Changing the scope

One of the more interesting features that we can perform with our scope names is to change them. We can also customize which modules to include on our use lines.

Altering the crate name

Normally, when we import a crate, we use the following:

```
extern crate crate_name;
```

However, to avoid confusion with something in your code, you may want to refer to the crate with a different name:

```
extern crate crate_name as my_crate;
```

It looks very similar to casting, which is because it casts the name `my_crate` to be `crate_name`.

When we now refer to the crate we don't use the following:

```
use crate_name::module;
```

We rather use the following:

```
use my_crate::module;
```

Optimizing your use statements

One of the very few things Java has done correctly is the degree of granularity in the way it imports libraries; it pushes the developer to only include the parts of the library actually required by the application. This is down to the history of Java, but it's something that should be encouraged. Rust does something similar.

The `use` statement can take a number of different styles.

The use-everything approach

This takes the following form:

```
use my_crate::module_name::*;
```

This is often referred to as the sledgehammer approach, as it makes available all the symbols (the functions, traits, and so on that are public) within the `module_name` scope. There is nothing wrong with this approach, but it ends up with a larger binary (which may slow down the final application and will certainly require more memory to run the code).

The you-decide approach

This is the very minimum required to use the `module_name` scope:

```
use my_crate::module_name;
```

Here, you are telling the compiler that `module_name` exists and that, as long as the function name exists in the symbols, it can be used. However, in order to use `module_name`, the function will need to be preceded by `module_name`. For example, to use the `print_me(f32)` function, which exists in `module_name`, you will have the following:

```
let some_text = module_name::print_me(10.1f32);
```

The `module_name::` has to be added to tell the compiler to use the `module_name` scope rather than the current scope of the application.

The use-me approach

Here, we tell the compiler that we are only allowing the current scope to use a specific function from within the `module_name` scope:

```
use my_crate::module_name::print_me;
```

The use-me-but-call-me-something-else approach

This is very similar to referring to the crate by another name:

```
use my_crate::module_name as mod_name;
```

This doesn't mean what you probably think it means. With the crate example, we said that we are going to use `my_crate`, which is the cast of `crate_name`. In this case, what we're saying is that `mod_name` is a cast of `my_crate::module_name`.

Let's use the following after the preceding line:

```
use my_crate::module_name;
let foo = module_name::print_me(10f32);
```

If we do so, we now use the following:

```
let foo = mod_name::print_me(10f32);
```

It looks the same, but really it means the following:

```
let foo = my_crate::module_name::print_me(10f32);
```

The use-glob approach

This approach is similar to the use-me approach, with the exception of using `{ }` around what we want the code to have access to (known as a **glob**):

```
use my_crate::module_name::{print_me, calculate_time};
```

The line means that the code can access `module_name::print_me` and `module_name::calculate_time` but nothing else from the `module_name` scope.

The use-glob-self approach

Here, the first parameter of the glob is `self`. In this context, `self` refers back to the root context:

```
use my_crate::module_name::{self, print as my_print, calculate as my_calc};
```

In an expanded form, this will equate to the following:

```
use my_crate::module_name;
use my_crate::module_name::print as my_print;
use my_crate::module_name::calculate as my_calc;
```

Summary

We covered a lot of ground in this chapter and saw that, for most of the time, cargo makes building a Rust application simple. When testing your own crates outside the project it was originally created in, we need to use `rustc` in order to compile. We saw how to create our own libraries, how to add unit tests, how to effectively utilize the use statement, and how to call crates and scopes by different names.

In our next chapter, we will be looking at how we can really make use of Rust's in-built memory protection system to fully utilize concurrency and parallelism.

11
Concurrency in Rust

Computers have come a long way in the last 35 years or so. Originally, we had the likes of the 6502, 6809, and Z80 processors. These were known as **single processing units**; they could only run a single program at a time and software ran in a linear fashion (this meant that performing two tasks at once wasn't possible).

Processors moved on, and from the single processing units (single-core), we moved on to processors that contained multiple processing units (multi-core). Programming languages evolved to allow for this form of processor, and running multiple operations (threads) at the same time became a reality.

Rust, being a very modern language, also has this ability to multiprocess. All of the benefits are available that you would expect from Rust (such as memory safety and avoiding race conditions), but there are some other things that you need to be aware of.

In this chapter, we will:

- Understand the mechanisms by which Rust performs concurrent processes
- Learn how to use threads
- See the difference between different threading models

A bit of a story

The Mystery Mobile was heading down a very dark road. There was no way of knowing what was ahead. At a certain point, they came to a point in the road with three roads coming off. Each road had a sign on them saying *Exit*. Being the intrepid type, Freddie sent Velma down one road, Shaggy and Scooby down the second and Daphne down the third. Being the brave sort, Freddie would drive down the road. They did know, though, that the roads would feed back into the main road at some point.

They agreed that whoever reached the exit first would send a message to the others. They synchronized their watches and moved off, not knowing who would reach the exit first or even if the exit could be reached at all.

What was that all about?

In roughly two paragraphs, I've illustrated three very important aspects of concurrency in Rust: **Send** (shown in the message being sent to the others from the Mystery Mobile), **Sync,** and **Threads** (each road donates a thread, and really, there is no real way to know when a thread will rejoin the sender, which can cause no ends of problems!).

Let's deal with each aspect in turn.

Send

Send transfers the type safely to another thread—in other words, if type T implements **Send**, then it means T has been passed safely to another thread.

There are a couple of caveats on using **Send**:

- You don't use it for a process that is not thread safe (such as FFI)
- Send has to be implemented for the type

Sync

Sync is considered the uber-safe option. When T implements **Sync**, there is a guarantee of memory safety. However, before we go any further, we need to consider the following question.

When is an immutable variable not an immutable variable?

Up to this point, we have considered variables to be either mutable or immutable, and that's it. However, this is not the case.

Consider the following:

```
let mut a = 10;
let b = &mut a;
```

What does this actually mean? First, we create a mutable binding to a that initially contains the value 10.

Next, we create an immutable binding to b that contains a reference to the mutable value of a.

And it's obviously mutable, it has mut in the definition

Let's consider a different example:

```
let vc: Vec<i32> = Vec::new();
let dup = vc.clone();
```

This example is not what it seems. When the clone trait is called, vc has to update its reference count. The problem is, vc is not mutable, yet this code compiles and runs.

To understand how, we have to know how the borrowing system works (for more information on borrowing, please refer to Chapter 8, *The Rust Application Lifetime*) in this instance. Borrowing has two very clear modes of operation:

- One (or more) references to the resource
- Exactly one mutable reference

Really, then, when we talk about immutability, we're not really talking about whether a variable is fixed, but whether it is safe to have more than one reference to the variable. In the preceding case, the mutation occurs within the vector structure and we have the &T from there.

As the vector structure is not user facing, it is called as **exterior mutable**.

Interior mutability

The opposite (interior mutability) can be found in this example:

```
use std::cell::RefCell;
fn main()
{
    let x = RefCell::new(42);
    let y = x.borrow_mut();
}
```

Here, `RefCell` gives the `&mut` when `borrow_mut()` is called. It works well, but will cause a panic if a second `borrow_mut()` is called on x; you are only allowed a single reference to a mutable.

Back to sync

For sync to occur, we cannot have any type that uses interior mutability (which also includes some of the primitive types).

When it comes to sharing across threads, Rust uses `Arc<T>`. This is a wrapper type that implements `send` and `sync` if the following condition is met: `T` must implement both `send` and `sync`. `RefCell` uses interior mutability, so `Arc<RefCell<T>>` won't implement `sync`, which also means `send` can't be used—therefore `RefCell` can't be passed around threads.

Using `send` and `sync` provides the strong guarantees of safety Rust relies upon to ensure the code is rock solid when using a threading system.

A beginner's guide to threading in Rust

Threads allow multiple processes to execute at the same time. The following is a very simple example of a threaded program:

```
use std::thread;
fn main()
{
    thread::spawn(||
    {
        println!("Hello from a thread in your Rust program");
    });
}
```

Code files can be found in `Chapter11/SimpleThreadExample`.

When compiled, you may expect the `println!` to show. However, what you get is this:

```
SimpleThreadExample — -bash — 80×5

Pauls-MacBook-Pro:SimpleThreadExample PFJ$ cargo run
     Running `target/debug/SimpleThreadExample`
Pauls-MacBook-Pro:SimpleThreadExample PFJ$
```

Figure 1

Why is the `println!` not showing?

An easy approach to thinking about how threads work.

Threads are more easily thought of graphically (at least I think so). We start with our main thread:

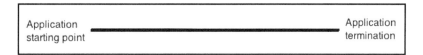

Figure 2

The main thread goes from the start of the application to the end of the application.

At any point on our main thread, we can create a new thread (or new threads, if required).

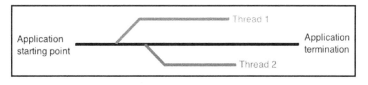

Figure 3

These two new threads can do anything the application needs them to do. There is a simple rule though: The threads can only last as long the application does. As *Figure 3* shows, the threads start and carry on their merry way; there is nothing to say the thread has to rejoin the main thread, nor is there any rule to say at what point the thread returns (which can cause some very large thread safety issues, leading to panics).

It goes without saying that each thread can also spawn their own threads to perform sub-processes:

Figure 4

If you're accustomed to threading in the likes of C, C++, and C#, you'll already know that a thread can return to the main thread at any time and that this *at any time* can be disastrous to the safe running of the application. It is different in Rust.

When a thread in Rust is spawned from either the main thread (or any subthread) a handle is created. Rust then uses this token to retrieve the thread at a given point; therefore, the issue of a race condition (where one thread returns before another, leading to crashes) is essentially removed.

Joining threads

To retrieve the spawned thread, Rust uses the `join()` trait and then unwraps the result.

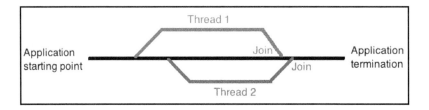

Figure 5

To make our small example application output, we therefore need to join the spawned thread back to the main thread:

```
use std::thread;
fn main()
{
    let threadhandle = thread::spawn(||
    {
        "Hello from a thread in your Rust program"
    });
    println!("{}", threadhandle.join().unwrap());
}
```

Code for the alterations can be found in `Chapter11/joined_thread`.

When we run the code, this time we see the following:

```
joined_thread — -bash — 80×7
Pauls-MacBook-Pro:joined_thread PFJ$ cargo run
    Running `target/debug/joined_thread`
Hello from a thread in your Rust program
Pauls-MacBook-Pro:joined_thread PFJ$
```

Figure 6

Hold on. That code isn't the same! This is true, and it is due to the spawn accepting a closure (| |).

Closures

Closures are a powerful piece of code present in many languages. Essentially, a closure wraps code or variables used only within the scope of the current code in a neat little package.

In its simplest form, we can have something like this:

```
let add = |x : i32 | x + t;
```

The part within the | | defines a variable called x that is only used within the scope of the calculation, and it is of type i32.

Okay, that may not seem that useful—after all, what we're doing here is adding two numbers together. Hold on though—if x is only defined within the scope of the calculation, what does x actually equal?

This is where closures come into their own. Typically, when we create a binding, we create a binding to something definite. Here, we are creating a binding, but binding it to the content of the closure. Anything between the pipes (| |) is an argument, with the expression being whatever follows the end pipe.

If you think about it, you've actually created something closer to the following:

```
fn add(x : i32) -> i32
{
    x + x
}
```

In answer to our question "what does x actually equal?", here it is equal to the only known parameter, t. Therefore, x + t is the same as saying t + t. The add variable isn't being bound directly (that is, in the same way that we bind under normal conditions), but is borrowing the binding. This means that we have to apply the same borrowing rules as before. Say that we have the following:

```
let m = &mut t;
```

This will give the following error:

```
   Compiling close_mut_error v0.1.0 (file:///Users/PFJ/Dropbox/Rust/Chapter%2011
%20-%20Concurrency/Code/close_mut_error)
src/main.rs:5:18: 5:19 error: cannot borrow `t` as mutable because it is also bo
rrowed as immutable [E0502]
src/main.rs:5      let m = &mut t;
                           ^

src/main.rs:4:15: 4:32 note:   previous borrow of `t` occurs here due to use in cl
osure; the immutable borrow prevents subsequent moves or mutable borrows of `t`
until the borrow ends
src/main.rs:4      let add = | x : i32 | x + t;

src/main.rs:6:2: 6:2 note:    previous borrow ends here
src/main.rs:2 {
src/main.rs:3      let mut t = 10i32;
src/main.rs:4      let add = | x : i32 | x + t;
src/main.rs:5      let m = &mut t;
src/main.rs:6 }

error: aborting due to previous error
Could not compile `close_mut_error`.
```

Figure 7

You will find an example of this error in `Chapter 11/close_mut_error`.

The important part of the throwback is that we're trying to borrow something that is being borrowed in an immutable line. We can fix this by changing the scope of the closure, as shown here:

```
let mut t = 10i32;
{
    let add = |x : i32 | x + t;
}
let m = &mut t;
```

This will result in the error going.

With that in mind, we can start to expand on this. If the value between the pipes is the argument, then we can clearly do some interesting things with closures

The code for this part can be found in `Chapter11/closures`.

Take this code, for example:

```
let calc = |x|
{
    let mut result: i32 = x;
    result *= 4;
    result += 2;
    result -= 1;
    result
};
```

Rather than create a whole new function, we use the closure and create the function inline with `result` and x only existing within the scope of the enclosure { }.

A closure without any arguments is the inline equivalent of the following:

```
fn do_something() -> T { ... }
```

Closures aren't all they first appear to be

Closures are known as **syntax sugar** (they effectively sweeten the bitterness of whatever they coat) for the underpinning trait they cover. This makes closures in Rust different to closures in other languages.

Given this premise, we can also use closures as arguments, as well as returning them from a function.

Closures as function arguments

Consider the following code:

```
fn call_with_three<F>(some_closure: F) -> i32 where F : Fn(i32) -> i32
{
some_closure(3)
}
fn main()
{
let answer = call_with_three(|x| x + 10 );
println!("{}", answer);
}
```

The code for this section can be found in `Chapter 11/close_fn_args`.

We call `call_with_three` and pass in the closure as the parameter. The function `call_with_three` takes a parameter of type `F`. So far, it's no different from any other function taking a generic value as an argument. However, we're binding `F` to be a function of type `i32`, which returns a value of type `i32`. We have created an inline function to be a parameter for a called function! When the code is compiled, we get the expected value on screen—**13**:

```
close_fn_args — -bash — 80×6
Pauls-MacBook-Pro:close_fn_args PFJ$ cargo run
   Compiling close_fn_args v0.1.0 (file:///Users/PFJ/Dropbox/Rust/Chapter%2011%2
0-%20Concurrency/Code/close_fn_args)
     Running `target/debug/close_fn_args`
13
Pauls-MacBook-Pro:close_fn_args PFJ$ 
```

Figure 8

Closures with explicit lifetimes – a special case

As we saw back in `Chapter 8`, *The Rust Application Lifetime*, there are two main types of scope: global and local. A variable that has a local scope goes out of bounds as soon as it is finished with, whereas a global scope variable is cleaned up when the application terminates. A global scope variable is also given the lifetime marker, `'`.

Closures also have different scopes. Typically, they will only be for the lifetime if they are called in, but they can also be global.

A "normal" function (as shown previously) would be as follows:

```
fn call_with_three<F>(some_closure: F) -> i32 where F : Fn(i32) -> i32
{
some_closure(3)
}
```

Conversely, for a lifetime scope, we would have the following:

```
fn call_with_three<'a, F>(some_closure: F) -> i32 where F : Fn(&'a 32) ->
i32
```

However, this won't compile. The problem is with the scope.

In our first example, the scope is purely for the lifetime of the invocation. In the second, it's for the lifetime of the function (and that is for the entirety of the function), which means that the compiler will see a mutable reference at the same lifetime as the immutable reference.

Although Rust does still allow us to use this, we need to use something called a **higher-ranked trait bounds** (in simple terms, it means that, in order of importance, this trumps something below it). This works by telling the compiler to use the minimum lifetime for the closure to run, which in turn should satisfy the borrow-checker. In this case, we use `for<...>`:

```
fn call_with_three<'a, F>(some_closure: F) -> i32 where F :<for 'a> Fn(&'a
32) -> i32
```

Returning a closure

As threads within Rust use a return from a closure, it makes sense for us to consider that it is entirely possible to return a closure. However, returning a closure is not as straightforward as you'd expect.

Let's consider a normal function first:

```
fn add_five(x : i32) -> i32
{
    return x + 5;
}
fn main()
{
    let test = add_five(5);
    println!("{}", test);
}
```

This will output the value 10. It's not rocket science. Let's change this to a closure:

```
fn add_five_closure() ->(Fn(i32)->i32)
{
    let num = 5;
    |x| x + num
}
fn main()
{
    let test = add_five_closure();
    let f = test(5);
    println!("{}", f);
}
```

The code for the example can be found in `Chapter 11/return_closure_one`.

When we run this, though, we don't get the expected answer of `10`—instead we get this:

```
 　　                return_closure_one — -bash — 80×34
   Compiling return_closure_one v0.1.0 (file:///Users/PFJ/Dropbox%20(Personal)/R ▣
ust/Chapter%2011%20-%20Concurrency/Code/return_closure_one)
src/main.rs:1:27: 1:39 error: the trait bound `std::ops::Fn(i32) -> i32 + 'stati
c: std::marker::Sized` is not satisfied [E0277]
src/main.rs:1 fn add_five_closeure() ->(Fn(i32)->i32){
                                        ^~~~~~~~~~~~~

src/main.rs:1:27: 1:39       : run `rustc --explain E0277` to see a detailed expla
nation
src/main.rs:1:27: 1:39       : `std::ops::Fn(i32) -> i32 + 'static` does not have
a constant size known at compile-time
src/main.rs:1:27: 1:39       : the return type of a function must have a staticall
y known size
src/main.rs:3:1: 3:12 error: mismatched types [E0308]
src/main.rs:3 |x| x + num
              ^~~~~~~~~~~

src/main.rs:3:1: 3:12        : run `rustc --explain E0308` to see a detailed explan
ation
src/main.rs:3:1: 3:12        : expected type `std::ops::Fn(i32) -> i32 + 'static`
src/main.rs:3:1: 3:12        :    found type `[closure@src/main.rs:3:1: 3:12 num:_]
`
src/main.rs:8:5: 8:9 error: the trait bound `std::ops::Fn(i32) -> i32: std::mark
er::Sized` is not satisfied [E0277]
src/main.rs:8 let test = add_five_closeure();
                         ^~~~

src/main.rs:8:5: 8:9        : run `rustc --explain E0277` to see a detailed explana
tion
src/main.rs:8:5: 8:9        : `std::ops::Fn(i32) -> i32` does not have a constant s
ize known at compile-time
src/main.rs:8:5: 8:9        : all local variables must have a statically known size
error: aborting due to 3 previous errors
error: Could not compile `return_closure_one`.

To learn more, run the command again with --verbose.
Pauls-MacBook-Pro:return_closure_one PFJ$ ▯
```

Figure 9

So what has gone wrong? When we return from a function, we have to tell the compiler the type we're returning. However, Fn is a trait, so we have to somehow satisfy this requirement. We could always have it return a reference:

```
fn add_five_closure() -> &(Fn(i32)->i32)
```

This will generate another compiler error as it needs a lifetime expectancy applied.

We could always make the function return a lifetime static reference:

```
fn add_five_closure() -> &'static (Fn(i32) → i32)
```

However, this will produce a different error, which may look somewhat confusing:

```
●  ●  ●              return_closure_two — -bash — 80×17
Pauls-MacBook-Pro:return_closure_two PFJ$ cargo run
    Compiling return_closure_two v0.1.0 (file:///Users/PFJ/Dropbox%20(Personal)/R
ust/Chapter%2011%20-%20Concurrency/Code/return_closure_two)
src/main.rs:3:1: 3:12 error: mismatched types [E0308]
src/main.rs:3 |x| x + num
                  ^~~~~~~~~~~
src/main.rs:3:1: 3:12 help: run `rustc --explain E0308` to see a detailed explan
ation
src/main.rs:3:1: 3:12 note: expected type `&'static std::ops::Fn(i32) -> i32 + '
static`
src/main.rs:3:1: 3:12 note:     found type `[closure@src/main.rs:3:1: 3:12 num:_]
`
error: aborting due to previous error
error: Could not compile `return_closure_two`.

To learn more, run the command again with --verbose.
Pauls-MacBook-Pro:return_closure_two PFJ$
```

Figure 10

Why are the types mismatched? It's expecting an i32, but has found a closure. Makes sense really, but why is this happening?

This is down to how Rust works. For a closure, it generates its own struct and implementation of Fn (and anything else required) therefore, we're dealing not with a literal, but something else.

Trying to return a trait object (such as Box) won't work either as the function relies on the num binding (which is stack allocated). However, if we move from the stack to the heap, we can now return the closure:

```
fn add_five_closure() -> Box<(Fn(i32) ->→ i32)>
{
    let num = 5;
    Box::new(move |x| x + num)
}
fn main()
{
    let test = add_five_closure();
    let f = test(5);
    println!("{}", f);
}
```

The source for this can be found in Chapter 11/return_closure_three.

This will now compile and give the following:

```
Pauls-MacBook-Pro:return_closure_three PFJ$ cargo run
   Compiling return_closure_three v0.1.0 (file:///Users/PFJ/Dropbox%20(Personal)
/Rust/Chapter%2011%20-%20Concurrency/Code/return_closure_three)
     Running `target/debug/return_closure_three`
10
```

Figure 11

What is the move parameter?

The move parameter forces the closure to take ownership of whatever is contained within. Let's look at that a bit closer:

```
let myNum = 10;
let myMove = move |x: i32| x + myNum;
```

Here, myMove takes ownership of myNum. The value of myNum implements Copy, which is assigned to the binding. This is the same as the operation of any variable, so there has to be something to differentiate move from anything else.

Let's look at a slightly different example and see if we can see what is actually going on:

```
let mut myMutNum = 10;
{
    let mut subNum = |x: i32| num -= x;
    subNum(3);
}
```

We've seen this before, so it should not be too hard to understand. This would give the answer 7. If we used move, however, the answer may not be as expected:

```
fn main()
{
    let mut my_mut_num = 10;
    {
        let mut sub_num = move |x: i32| my_mut_num -= x;
        sub_num(3);
    }
    println!("{}", my_mut_num);
}
```

The code for this example is in Chapter 11/move_closure_one.

When compiled, you may expect the answer 7, but instead you get:

```
Pauls-MacBook-Pro:move_closure_one PFJ$ cargo run
   Compiling move_closure_one v0.1.0 (file:///Users/PFJ/Dropbox%20(Personal)/Rus
t/Chapter%2011%20-%20Concurrency/Code/move_closure_one)
     Running `target/debug/move_closure_one`
10
```

Figure 12

How can we have a value of 10?

In the nonmove version, we borrow the value of the mutable. With move, we take ownership of a copy. In practical terms, we have created a completely new stack frame for the closure. The sub_num() call is still being executed, but when it is called, the value returned is not the expected one, but the ownership of the copy of the original value (10).

Back to threading

Now we have seen how closures work and their importance, we can continue with threading.

If we consider *Figure 5*, we can use a closure to return a value from one of the subthreads:

```
use std::thread;
fn main()
{
    let x = 10;
    thread::spawn(|| (println!("x is {}", x); ));
}
```

Will this work as is? Unfortunately not. We are borrowing x, which we can't do because of ownership problems. However, we could add move to the invocation:

```
use std::thread;
fn main()
{
    let x = 10;
    thread::spawn(move || (println!("x is {}", x); ));
}
```

The thread will take ownership of the copy of x rather than borrow the value. By taking ownership, Rust prevents a common issue with any form of threading: race conditions. If you recall, from the start of this chapter I said that conventional threading has no guarantees of when a thread will return, which can cause all sorts of issues. Typically, other languages use mutexes to try and prevent the race condition (mutex stands for mutual exclusion, which should give an idea as to how they work). By taking ownership, Rust does a lot to prevent racing.

Ownership has its advantages

With the Rust ownership system, we can largely negate what many other languages have issues with, that of shared mutable states. Developers in other languages would usually rather chew off their legs than have to deal with a shared mutable state; they're inherently problematic—how can you share a mutable and not have problems with the return of the thread?

Rust doesn't have this issue, as the shared part is sorted with the ownership system.

The reference counter

Consider the following piece of code. It won't work because there are multiple owners of the `vec`:

```
use std::thread;
use std::time::Duration;
fn main()
{
    let mut my_data = vec![5, 8, 13];
    for i in 0..10
    {
        thread::spawn(move || { my_data[0] += i; }); // fails here
    }

    thread::sleep(Duration::from_millis(50));
}
```

There has to be a way to get this compile, and there is. Rust provides us with a reference counter called `Rc`. The reference count has to have a type associated with it, and so it is commonly quoted as `Rc<T>`. This can be used to keep track of each reference. Every time we execute a clone on the execution, the reference count is incremented (and a new owned reference created), so the compiler always knows when something is returned.

The only problem with using `Rc<T>` is that it doesn't implement send. Therefore, we use `Arc<T>` (the `A` stands for atomic—it is Rust's own reference count and can be accessed across threads).

`Arc<T>`, though, has its own problem: by default, the contents are immutable. You can share data with `Arc<T>`, but *shared* mutable values—that's a different matter. Mutable shared values give rise to race conditions and that is what we are most certainly not after.

There are alternatives to `Arc<T>` (namely `RefCell<T>` and `Cell<T>`, but neither of these implement sync, and so they can't be used with threading).

Problem solved – use Mutex

Rust provides us with `Mutex<T>`. This works in much the same way as other languages by locking the thread. We implement `mutex` in our code like this:

```
use std::sync::{Arc, Mutex};
use std::thread;
use std::time::Duration;
fn main()
```

```
{
    let primes = Arc::new(Mutex::new(vec![1,2,3,5,7,9,13,17,19,23]));

    for i in 0..10
    {
        let primes = primes.clone();
        thread::spawn(move ||
        {
            let mut data = primes.lock().unwrap();
            data[0] += i;
        });
    }
    thread::sleep(Duration::from_millis(50));
}
```

The code for this example is in `Chapter 11/mutex`.

By using `lock`, we only allow a single thread to have access to that data at any one time (it has mutual exclusion). No other thread has access to that value, and if any other thread tries to access the value, it has to wait until the lock is released. When data goes out of scope (when i is incremented), the lock is released.

Why do we put the thread to sleep?

Usually, the use of `thread::sleep` allows the execution to pause for a finite amount of time as an extra protection against racing. This is not always a good plan as there isn't any real way to tell how long a thread is going to take, so it's at best a guess. As with all guesses, they can be wildly inaccurate (it is used here as we're not doing anything with the data value).

In real systems, the preferred method, to ensure that the correct amount of time is given to ensure that everything has worked is to synchronize the threads using channels.

Thread synchronization

The best way to think of a channel is to see it as a walkie-talkie. At one end you have the transmitter (send) and at the other end, the receiver:

```
use std::thread;
use std::sync::mpsc;

fn main() {
    // tx = transmission = sender
    // rx = receiver
    let (tx, rx) = mpsc::channel();

    for i in 0..10
    {
        let tx = tx.clone();

        thread::spawn(move ||
        {
            let answer = (i * 2) * i;

            tx.send(answer).unwrap();
        });
    }

    for _ in 0..10
    {
        println!("{}", rx.recv().unwrap());
    }
}
```

 The code for this example is in Chapter 11/channels.

When we run this, we get the following:

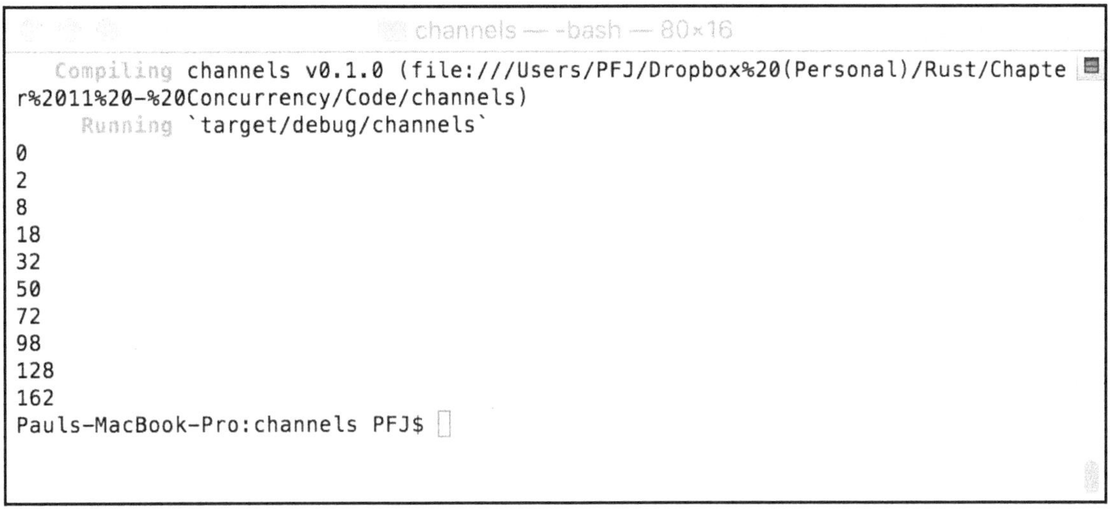

```
channels — -bash — 80×16
    Compiling channels v0.1.0 (file:///Users/PFJ/Dropbox%20(Personal)/Rust/Chapte
r%2011%20-%20Concurrency/Code/channels)
     Running `target/debug/channels`
0
2
8
18
32
50
72
98
128
162
Pauls-MacBook-Pro:channels PFJ$ 
```

Figure 13

Thread panics

As with anything in Rust (and pretty much any language), things can go wrong and the application will throw a panic. As with any other time a panic occurs, we can use panic! to catch the panic and then test the result to see if the thread did indeed panic. We do this using a construct such as:

```
let handle = thread::spawn(move || { panic! ("panic occurred"); });
let res = handle.join();
```

The join() will return Result<T, E>, which can then be checked to see if there is an exception.

Summary

We have seen in this chapter how Rust deals with threading within an application. Be under no illusion of the power threading has and the inherent issues it gives rise to. However, when used correctly, threading can greatly improve the performance of your application. Think of a web browser if you need further proof; imagine the speed of one if everything was performed on a single thread—a simple page could take over a minute to render!

We have also looked at closures and the power behind them. Put the two together and you can appreciate how powerful threading and inline functions can be.

We're taking a break in the next chapter to access how your Rust skills are progressing with another project task that will build upon the ones performed in `Chapter 6`, *Creating Your Own Rust Applications*. After that, we'll be concluding the book with a look at the standard libraries and using external libraries to further improve your Rust applications by interfacing with them.

12
Now It's Your Turn!

We're rapidly approaching the end of the book and it is time for you to put what we've covered and you've learned into practice. As with Chapter 6, *Creating Your Own Rust Applications*, this chapter will take the form of a number of challenges for you. There is no sample code for this chapter, so it's all down to you. The majority of the challenges will be based around the mathlib library covered in Chapter 10, *Creating Your Own Crate*, as well as using code created in Chapter 6, *Creating Your Own Rust Applications*.

Task 1 – cleaning the code (part 1)

If you consider the code examples in temperature.rs, you will see that some use a tuple and some use a single type return. While for development this is a fairly acceptable approach, for a release we may want something more structured.

Consider the two functions kelvin_to_celcius and celcius_to_farenheit; in order to use them, we need to have two variables:

```
let ktoc = kelvin_to_celcius(14.5f32);
let ctof = celcius_to_fahrenheit(24.3f32);
```

There are a number of possible solutions to this problem.

- Do nothing! Many libraries use multiple variables when the function returns different types.
- Implement a trait within the module that tests the return for false and returns either a String containing the answer or *calculation failed*.

- Define a single `struct` for the answer of the form, which is then passed back to the caller, as follows:

```
pub struct maths_answersMathsAnswers {
    calc_complete : bool,
    fanswer : f32,
    ianswer : i32,
}
```

If we remove the first option (after all, what would be the point in doing this as part of a chapter given over to testing what we have covered?), we are left with options 2 - 4 or 3.

The problems with each option

Each option has its own unique associated problems.

The String option

The issue with the second option is that, if we return a `String` and then want to do something else with the answer (possibly a further calculation from one of the other modules within the crate), we will need some method of converting the string (after checking it doesn't contain the error code) back to an `f32` to pass into the second function.

The struct option

The problem with the third option is that, when we call within the library, we either have a return type of `tuple(bool, f32)` or `f32`. Therefore, in a function that only returns a single type, we will need to set `calc_completed` to `true`.

It is possible to set a default value on the `struct` by deriving or implementing `std::Default` (we will cover the standard library in Chapter 13, *The Standard Library*, and Chapter 14, *Foreign Function Interfaces*). Here's a derived version:

```
#[derive(Default)]
pub struct MathsAnswers {
    calc_complete : bool,
    fanswer : f32,
    ianswer : i32,
}
```

All primitive types in Rust have a sensible default value: numbers are zeroes, bool is false, Strings are empty strings, and so on. The preceding code is equivalent to the following manually implemented `Default`:

```
impl Default for MathsAnswers {
  fn default () -> MathsAnswers {
    MathsAnswers {calc_complete: false, fanswer: 0f32, ianswer: 0i32 }
  }
}
```

However, we want the calc_complete default to be true, so we'll use this implementation instead:

```
impl Default for MathsAnswers {
  fn default () -> MathsAnswers {
    MathsAnswers {calc_complete: false, fanswer: 0f32, ianswer: 0i32 }
  }
}
```

After the `Default` implementation, we may choose to only fill in some of the values when creating an instance and supply `Default::default()` for the rest:

```
// do calculation then
let answers =  MathsAnswers { fanswer: calc_ans, ..Default::default() };
return MathsAnswers;
```

The potential problem is where to put the struct in terms of scope. Where would it be best to place it?

The task

You are to decide which one of the options for refactoring the code would work best and then implement it. You should create a number of unit tests to ensure the sanity checks work and then test it in your own test rig application to ensure nothing has broken with the crate and scope.

Task 2 – cleaning the code (part 2)

While each function is kept apart in the crate, we can always clean up the code to make it safer (we have a single public function and keep the calculations away from prying eyes).

The task

Each function takes a single parameter of either the `f32` or `i32` type and thankfully, we can separate out the modules to be those that return an `f32` or `i32` (the bases all return `i32`: all of the others have their answers in `f32`).

If we look at the temperatures module, everything will return the answer as `f32` (after task 1, how it does this is up to you). We can therefore create a single function that takes as the first parameter the conversion to be performed and as the second the value.

When the single function recognizes the first parameter, it calls the now private functions and returns the value.

As with the first task, you will need to implement this and create documentation for the new library. You should create a new unit test for the crate and test it in your test rig application.

Task 3 – extending the crate (part 1)

You will have noticed that, in the example library, there is no code at all for the `regression_analysis` module. This is deliberate.

Back in `Chapter 6`, *Creating Your Own Rust Applications*, one of the tasks was to create code that enabled you to perform a regression analysis based on formulae provided. The code created can now be firmly split into two parts:

- The equation for the straight line, $y = mx + c$, which will also give the intercepts on the x and y axis
- The standard deviation and regression analysis

The task

In this task, you are to take your code and put it into the `mathslib` crate. This may not be as simple as it seems. The library will need to take:

- A filename for the file containing the data
- A vector containing either a `struct` or `tuple` that holds the data

However, the problem doesn't lie in the data, but rather in the fact that, each time a calculation is made, the whole regression analysis has to be performed. For example, to calculate the standard deviation, you can't just pass in the results for the equation of a straight line—that won't work, but will cause the whole calculation to be performed again.

In terms of the speed of a library, this is very inefficient; you should calculate once and be able to draw out all answers from there. In terms of your code, this will require some re-organization.

Once you have done this, you should create the unit tests for each function and test them in your test rig app with both a vector then the filename.

You will need to add the documentation for this task to your current documentation.

Task 4 – extending the crate (part 2)

By now, you will have a firm grasp of how crates work, the required testing regime, and creating a test rig. Your final task in this section is to create your own extension to the crate. There are some criteria though to your extension:

- One of the functions must return a non-primitive type
- The calculations should be private; there should be some form of interface to the function call
- There should be a single function that takes an XML file as a parameter to perform the calculation
- The new module must be fully documented and complete with its own tests

Summary

We've finished the main part of the book. We've covered the majority of the Rust language and these end-of-section chapters should have helped you consolidate your knowledge.

In the final part of the book, we'll cover the standard libraries and how to interface your Rust application to an external library.

13
The Standard Library

As with all programming languages, Rust comes with a rich library to make the life of the developer that much simpler by providing frequently-used functionality without having to recode the same thing time and again. We have already encountered part of the standard library in this book, and I have no doubt that you will have seen any number of instances of it in other code examples.

Over the next two chapters, we will be looking at what the library provides and how to use it.

In this chapter, we will be dealing with the standard crate (`std::`).

Chapter format

Unlike the other chapters in this book, due to the sheer size of the library this chapter will be slightly different. It will look like this:

Trait name

What it does / provides

Notes

Traits / Structs and Enums provided

Download example

Due to Rust also having two main variants (stable and unstable), I won't be covering anything that is currently classed as unstable within the library; there is no guarantee that it will remain in the library or will remain the same.

What is the standard library?

The standard library contains the core functionality for Rust. It is split into four parts:

- The standard modules
- Primitive types
- Macros
- Prelude

The standard modules (overview)

The standard modules implement the likes of string handling, IO, network, and operating system calls. There are around 60 of these modules in total. Some are self-contained while others provide implementations for traits and structs.

The module names may give rise to some confusion as they share the same name with a primitive type (such as `i32`).

Primitive types (overview)

Primitive types are those types that are provided for us. In other languages, they would be the likes of `int`, `float`, and `char`. In Rust, we have `i32`, `d32`, and `i8` (respectively). Rust provides the developer with 19 primitives, some of which will provide additional implementations.

Macros (overview)

Macros play a significant role in Rust application development; they have been designed to provide a number of very convenient shortcuts to avoid the pain of having to implement common functionality (such as `println!(...)` and `format!(...)`). Rust provides 30 macros.

Prelude

Prelude is very useful. You may have wondered why many of the examples in this book use standard modules, but you rarely see `use std::` at the top of source files. The reason is that Rust auto-injects the prelude module into every source file, which provides the source file with a number of core modules. It inserts the following in no particular order:

- `std::marker::{Copy, Send, Sized, Sync}`
- `std::ops::{Drop, Fn, FnMut, FnOnce}`
- `std::mem::drop`
- `std::boxed::Box`
- `std::borrow::ToOwned`
- `std::clone::Clone`
- `std::cmp::{PartialEq, PartialOrd, Eq, Ord }`
- `std::convert::{AsRef, AsMut, Into, From}`
- `std::default::Default`
- `std::iter::{Iterator, Extend, IntoIterator, DoubleEndedIterator, ExactSizeIterator}`
- `std::option::Option::{self, Some, None}`
- `std::result::Result::{self, Ok, Err}`
- `std::slice::SliceConcatExt`
- `std::string::{String, ToString}`
- `std::vec::Vec`

It inserts into each crate `extern crate std;` and into each module `use std::prelude::v1::*;`. This is all that is needed for prelude - it is that simple! Each module, though, will be dealt with in turn.

The standard modules

With the overviews done, let's look at the standard modules.

std::Any

This module enables the dynamic casting of `'static` via runtime reflection.

 It can be used to obtain a `TypeId`. When used as a borrowed trait reference (`&Any`), it can be used to determine whether the value is a given type (using `Is`) and also to get a reference to the inner value as a type (using `downcast_ref`). `&mut Any` will allow access to `downcast_mut`, which obtains the mutable reference to the inner value. `&Any` can only be used for testing a specific type and cannot be used to test whether a type implements a trait.

Structs

- `TypeId`: `TypeId` is an opaque object that cannot be examined, but does allow for clone, compare, print, and show. Only available for types that use `'static`.

Implement

- `of<T>() -> TypeId where T:'static + Reflect + ?Sized`: This returns the `TypeId` of the type `T` the function was instantiated with.

Traits

- `pub trait Any: 'static + Reflect {fn get_type_id(&self) -> TypeId; }`: Emulates dynamic typing.

Trait methods

- `impl Any + 'static`
    - `is<T>(&self) -> bool where T:Any`: Returns `true` if the boxed type is the same as `T`
    - `downcast_ref<T>(&self) -> Option<&T> where T:Any`: Returns `ref` to the boxed value whether it is of type `T` or `None`
    - `downcast_mut<T>(&mut self) -> Option<&mut T> where T:Any`: As for `downcast_ref` but returns a mutable `ref` or `None`

- `impl Any + 'static + Send`
  - `is<T>(&self) -> bool where T:Any`: Sends to the method defined on the type `Any`
  - `downcast_ref<T>(&self) -> Option<&T> where T:Any`: Sends to the method defined on the type `Any`
  - `downcast_mut<T>(&mut self) -> Option<&mut T> where T:Any`: Sends to the method defined on the type `Any`

Trait implementations

- `impl Debug for Any + 'static`
  - `fmt(&self, f: &mut Formatter) -> Result<(), Error>`: Format the value using the formatter
- `impl Debug for Any + 'static + Send`
  - `fmt(&self, f: &mut Formatter) -> Result<(), Error>`: Sends to the method defined on the `Debug` method

std::ascii

This module performs operations on ASCII strings.

 The `AsciiExt` trait contains a number of useful string slice utilities for testing, as well as conversion to upper and lowercase.

Structs

- `pub struct EscapeDefault`: Iterates over the escaped version of a byte
- `impl` iterator for `EscapeDefault`
  - `type Item = u8`: Type of the elements iterated over
- `impl` iterator for `EscapeDefault` functions
  - `next(&mut self) -> Option<u8>`: Advances the iterator and return the next value
  - `size_hint(&self) -> (usize, Option<usize>)`: Returns the bounds on the remaining length of the iterator
  - `count(self) -> usize`: Returns the number of iterations

- `last(self) -> Option<Self::Item>`: Returns the last element
- `nth(&mut self, n:usize) -> Option<Self::Item>`: Returns the next element after the nth position
- `chain<U>(self, other:U) -> Chain<Self, U::IntoIterator> where U: IntoIterator<Item=Self::Item>`: Takes two iterators and creates a new one over both in sequence
- `zip<U>(self, other: U) -> Zip<Self, U:IntoIterator> where U:IntoIterator`: Takes two iterators and makes them into a single pair iterator
- `map<T,U>(self, u: U) -> Map<Self, U> where U:FnMut(Self::Item) -> T`: Creates an iterator from a closure that calls that closure on each element
- `filter<F>(self, predicate: F) -> Filter<Self, F> where F: FnMut(&Self::Item) -> bool`: Creates an iterator that uses a closure to determine whether an element should be returned
- `enumerate(self) -> Enumerate<Self>`: Gives the current iteration count and the next value
- `peekable(self) -> Peekable<Self>`: Peeks at the next value without the iterator consuming it
- `skip_while<P>(self, predicate:P) -> SkipWhile<Self, P> where P:FnMut(&Self::Item) -> bool`: Creates an iterator that skips *n* elements based on the predicate.
- `take_while<P>(self, predicate:P) -> TakeWhile<Self, P> where P:FnMut(&Self::Item) -> bool`: Creates an iterator that yields elements based on the predicate.
- `skip(self, n: usize) -> Skip<Self>`: Skips the first *n* elements
- `take(self, n: usize) -> Take<Self>`: The iterator that yields the first *n* elements
- `scan<S, T, U>(self, interal_state: S, u: U) -> Scan<Self, S, U> where U:FnMut(&mut S, Self::Item)-> Option<T>`: The iterator adapter that holds an internal state and produces a new iterator

- `flat_map<T, U>(self, u:U) -> Flat_Map<Self, T, U> where U:FnMut(Self::Item) -> T, T:IntoIterator:` Creates an iterator that works like a map, but produces a flattened, nested structure
- `fuse(self)->Fuse(Self):` Iterator that terminates after the first instance of `None`
- `inspect<T>(self, t: T)->Insepect<Self, T> where T: FnMut(&self::Item)->():` Does something with each iterated element and passes the value on.
- `by_ref(&mut self) -> &mut Self:` Borrows rather than consumes the iterator
- `collect<T>(self) -> T where T:FromIterator(Self::Item):` Makes a collection from an iterator
- `partition<T, U>(self, u:U) -> (T,T) where T:Default + Extend<Self::Item>, U:FnMut(&Self::Item> -> bool:` Takes the iterator and creates two collections from it
- `fold<T, U>(self, init:T, u:U)->T where U:FnMut(T, Self::Item) -> T:` The iterator adapter that applies a function to produce a single final result
- `all<T>(&mut self, t:T) -> bool where T:FnMut(Self::Item) -> bool:` Tests whether all elements of the iterator match the predicate `T`
- `any<T>(&mut self, t:T) -> bool where T:FnMut(Self::Item) -> bool:` Tests whether any elements of the iterator match the predicate `T`
- `find<T>(&mut self, predicate:T) -> Option<Self::Item> where T: FnMut(&Self::Item) -> bool:` Searches the iterator for a match to the predicate
- `position<T>(&mut self, predicate:T) -> Option<usize> where T:FnMut(Self::Item) -> bool:` Searches the iterator for a match to the predicate and return the index
- `rposition<T>(&mut self, predicate:T) -> Option<usize> where T:FnMut(Self::Item) -> bool, Self:ExtractSizeIterator + doubleEndedIterator:` As for position, except it searches from the right
- `max(self_ => Option<Self::Item>:` Returns the max element of the iterator

- `min(self_ => Option<Self::Item>`: Returns the min element of the iterator
- `rev(self) -> Rev<Self> where Self:DoubleEndedIterator`: Reverses the direction of the iterator
- `unzip<T, U, FromT, FromU>(self) -> (FromT, FromU) -> Where FromT: Default + Extend<T>, FromU: Default + Extend<U>, Self::Iterator<Item=(T,U)>`: Performs the reverse of ZIP (two collections from a single iterator)
- `cloned<'a, Y>(self) -> Cloned<Self> where Self:Iterator<Item = &'a T>, T: 'a + Clone`: Creates an iterator that clones all of its elements
- `cycle(self) -> Cycle<Self> where Self:Clone`: Repeats the iterator endlessly
- `sum<T>(self) -> T where Y:Add<Self::Item, Output=T> + Zero`: Returns the sum of the iterator elements
- `Product<T>(self) -> T where T: Mul<Self::Item, Output = T> + One`: Multiplies the elements of the iterator and returns the value

- `impl DoubleEndedIterator for EscapeDefault`
  - `next_back(&mut self) -> Option<u8>`: Iterator able to yield a result from both ends
- `impl ExactSizeIterator for EscapeDefault`
  - `Len(&self) -> usize`: Returns the number of times the iterator will iterate.

Traits

```
pub trait AsciiExt {
  type Owned;
  fn is_ascii(&self) -> bool ;
  fn to_ascii_uppercase(&self) -> Self:: Owned ;
  fn to_ascii_lowercase(&self) -> Self:: Owned ;
  fn eq_ignore_ascii_case(&self, other: &Self) -> bool ;
  fn make_ascii_uppercase(&mut self);
  fn make_ascii_lowercase(&mut self);
}
```

The following are extension methods for ASCII subset operations on string slices:

- Associated type
    - `Owned`: Container for copied ASCII characters.
- Required methods
    - `is_ascii(&self) -> bool`: Whether value is an ASCII value
    - `to_ascii_uppercase(&self) -> Self::Owned`: Makes a copy of the string in ASCII uppercase
    - `to_ascii_lowercase(&self) -> Self::Owned`: As for uppercase, but in lowercase
    - `eq_ignore_ascii_case(&self, other: &Self) -> bool`: Are two strings the same ignoring the case

std::borrow

This module is used for working with borrowed data.

enum `Cow` (clone-on-write smarter pointer)

The `Cow` allows for immutable access to borrowed data (and can enclose this data) and permits cloning lazily when mutation or ownership is required. It is designed to work using the `Borrow` trait. It also implements `Deref`, which will allow access to non-mutating methods on the data `Cow` has enclosed. `to_mut` will provide a mutable reference to the owned value.

- Trait `std::borrow::Borrow`: Data can be borrowed in a number of different ways: shared borrowing (`T` and `&T`), mutable borrowing (`&mut T`), and borrowed slices from the likes of `Vec<T>` (`&[T]`, and `&mut [T]`).
  The `Borrow` trait provides a convenient method to abstract over the given type. For example: `T: Borrow<U>` means that `&U` is borrowed from `&T`
    - `fn borrow(&self) -> &Borrowed`: Immutably borrows from an owned value
- Trait `std::borrow::BorrowMut`: Used for mutably borrowing data
    - `fn borrow_mut(&mut self) -> &mut Borrowed`: Mutably borrows from an owned value

- Trait `std::borrow:ToOwned`: A generalization of `Clone` for borrowing data. `Clone` only works when going from `&T` to `T`. `ToOwned` generalizes `Clone` to construct owned data from any borrow of a given type.

    - `fn to_owned(&self) -> Self::Owned`: Creates owned data from borrowed data

std::boxed

This module is used for heap allocation.

 A very simple way to allocate memory on the heap, provide ownership, and drop when out of scope.

- `impl<T> Box<T>`
    - `fn new(x:T) -> Box<T>`: Allocates memory on the heap and places `x` into it
- `impl <T> Box<T> where T: ?Sized`
    - `unsafe fn from_raw(raw: *mut T) -> Box<T>`: Constructs a box from a raw pointer. After creation, the pointer is owned by the new `Box`. It is unsafe for this very reason; the `Box` destructor will call the destructor of `T` and free the allocated memory. This may lead to double freeing that will cause a crash.
    - `fn into_raw(b: Box<T> -> *mut T`: Consumes the box and returns the wrapped raw pointer.
- `impl Box<Any + 'static>`
    - `fn downcast<T>(self) -> Result<Box<T>, Box<Any + 'static>>` where `T:Any`: Attempts to downcast the box to a concrete type.
- `impl Box<Any + 'static + Send>`
    - `fn downcast<T>(self) -> Result<Box<T>, Box<Any + 'static + Send>>` where `T:Any`: Attempts to downcast the box to a concrete type

Methods

Trait Implementations

- `Impl <T> Default for Box<T> where T:Default`
    - `fn default() -> Box<T>`: Returns the default value for the type
- `impl<T> Default for Box<[T]>`
    - `fn default() -> Box<T>`: Returns the default value for the type
- `impl<T> Clone for Box<T> where T:Clone`
    - `fn clone(&self) -> Box<T>`: Returns a new box with a clone of the box's contents
    - `fn clone_from(&mut self, source: &Box<T>)`: Copies *sources* contents into self without creating a new allocation
- `impl Clone for Box<str>`
    - `fn clone(&self) -> Box<str>`: Returns a copy of the value
    - `fn clone_from(&mut self, source: &Self)`: Performs a copy-assignment from *source*
- `impl<T> PartialEq<Box<T>> for Box<T> where T:PartialEq<T> + ?Sized`
    - `fn eq(&self, other: &Box<T>) -> bool`: Test self and other to be equal. Used by ==
    - `fn ne(&self, other: &Box<T>) ->`: Tests for inequality. Used by !=
- `impl<T> PartialOrd<Box<T>> for Box<T> where T:PartialOrd<T> + ?Sized`
    - `fn partial_cmp(&self, other: &Box<T>) -> Option<Ordering>`: Returns an ordering between self and other values if it exists
    - `fn lt(&self, other: &Box<T>) -> bool`: Tests whether self is less than other. Used by <
    - `fn le(&self, other: &Box<T>) -> bool`: Tests whether self is less than or equal to other. Used by <=
    - `fn ge(&self, other: &Box<T>) -> bool`: Tests whether self is greater than or equal to other. Used by >=
    - `Fn gt(&self, other: &Box<T>) -> bool`: Tests whether self is greater than other. Used by >

- `impl <T> Ord for Box<T> where T:Ord + ?Sized`
  - `fn cmp(&self, other: &Box<T>) -> Ordering`: Returns an ordering between self and other
- `impl <T> Hash for Box<T> where T: Hash + ?Sized`
  - `fn hash<H>(&self, state: &mut H) where H: Hasher`: Feeds the value into the state and updates the hasher if required
  - `fn hash_slice<H>(data: &[Self], state &mut H) where H: Hasher`: Feeds the slice of this type into the state
- `impl<T> From<T> for Box<T>`
  - `fn from(t: T) -> Box<T>`: Performs a conversion
- `impl<T> Display for Box<T> where T: Display + ?Sized`
  - `fn fmt(&self, f: &mut Formatter) -> Result<(), Error>`: Formats the value using the given formatter
- `impl<T> Debug for Box<T> where T:Debug + ?Sized`
  - `fn fmt(&self, f: &mut Formatter) -> Result<(), Error>`: Formats the value using the given formatter
- `impl<T> Pointer for Box<T> where T: ?Sized`
  - `fn fmt(&self, f: &mut Formatter) -> Result<(), Error>`: Formats the value using the given formatter
- `impl<T> Deref for Box<T> where T: ?Sized`
  - `fn deref(&self) -> &T`: Dereference a value
- `impl<T> DerefMut for Box<T> where T: ?Sized`
  - `fn deref_mut(&mut self) -> &mut T`: Mutably dereference a value
- `impl<I> Iterator for Box<I> where I: Iterator + ?Sized`
  - `fn next(&mut self) -> Option<I::Item>`: Advances the iterator and returns the next value
  - `fn size_hint(&self) -> (usize, Option<usize>)`: Returns the bounds on the remaining length of the iterator
  - `fn count(self) -> usize`: Returns the number of iterations
  - `fn last(self) -> Option<Self::Item>`: Returns the last element
  - `fn nth(&mut self, n: usize) -> Option<Self::Item>`: Consumes *n* elements of the iterator and returns the next one after that

- `fn chain<U>(self, other: U) -> Chain<Self, U::Iterator> where U: IntoIterator <Item=Self::Item>`: Takes two iterators and creates a new one over both in sequence
- `fn zip<U>(self, other: U) -> Zip<Self, U::IntoIter> where U: IntoIter`: Zips two iterators into a single pair
- `fn map<B, F>(self, f: F) -> Map<Self, F> where F: FnMut(Self::Item) -> B`: Takes a closure and creates an iterator that calls that closure on each element
- `fn filter<P>(self, predicate: P) -> Filter<Self, P> where P: FnMut(&Self::Item) -> bool`: Creates an iterator that uses a closure to see if an element should be yielded
- `Fn filter_map<B, F>(self, f: F) -> FilterMap<Self, F> where F: FnMut(Self::Item) -> Option<B<`: Creates an iterator that filters and maps
- `fn enumerate(self) -> Enumerate<Self>`: Creates an iterator that gives the current iteration count and the next value
- `fn peekable(self) -> Peekable<Self>`: Creates an iterator to peek at the next element of the iterator without consuming
- `fn skip_while<P>(self, predicate: P)-> SkipWhile<Self, P> where P: FnMut(&Self::Item) -> bool`: Creates an iterator that skips elements based on the predicate
- `fn skip(self, n: usize) -> Skip<Self>`: Creates an iterator that skips the first *n* elements
- `fn take(self, n:usize) -> Take<Self>`: Creates an iterator that yields the first *n* elements
- `fn take_while<P>(self, predicate: P) -> TakeWhile<Self. P> where P:FnMut(&Self::Item) -> bool`: Creates an iterator that yields elements based on the predicate
- `fn scan<St, B, F>(self, init_state: St, f : F) -> Scan<Self, St, F> where F: FnMut(&mut St, Self::Item) -> Option<B>`: An iterator adaptor similar to `fold()` that holds the internal state and produces a new iterator
- `fn flat_map<U, F>(self f: F) -> FlatMap<Self, U, F> where F: FnMut(Self::Item) -> U, U:IntoIterator`: Creates a flattened nested structure. Works like map.

- `fn fuse(self) -> Fuse<Self>`: Creates an iterator that ends after the first instance of `None`
- `fn inspect<F>(self, f: F) -> Inspect<Self, F> where F:FnMut(&Self::Item) -> ()`: Does something with each element and passes the value on
- `fn by_ref(&mut self) -> &mut Self`: Borrow the iterator. Doesn't consume it.
- `fn collect<B>(self) -> B where B: FromIterator <Self::Item>`: Changes the iterator to a collection
- `fn partition<B, F>(self, f: F) -> (B, B) where B: Default + Extend<Self::Item>, F: FnMut(&Self::Item) -> bool`: Consumes an iterator, creating two collections from it
- `fn fold<B, F>(self, init: B, f: F) -> B where F: FnMut(B, Self::Item) -> B`: An iterator adaptor that applies a function, producing a single, final value
- `fn all<F>(&mut self, f: F) -> bool where F: FnMut(Self::Item) -> bool`: Tests if every element of the iterator matches a predicate
- `fn any<F>(&mut self, f: F) -> bool where F: FnMut(Self::Item) -> bool`: Tests if any element of the iterator matches a predicate
- `fn find<P>(&mut self, predicate: P) -> Option<Self::Item> where P: FnMut(&Self::Item) -> bool`: Searches for an element of an iterator that satisfies a predicate
- `fn position<P>(&mut self, predicate: P) -> Option<usize> where P: FnMut(Self::Item) -> bool`: Searches for an element in an iterator, returning its index
- `fn rposition<P>(&mut self, predicate: P) -> Option<usize> where P: FnMut(Self::Item) -> bool, Self: ExactSizeIterator + DoubleEndedIterator`: Searches for an element in an iterator from the right, returning its index
- `fn max(self) -> Option<Self::Item> where Self::Item: Ord`: Returns the maximum element of an iterator
- `fn min(self) -> Option<Self::Item> where Self::Item: Ord`: Returns the minimum element of an iterator

- `fn max_by_key<B, F>(self, f: F) -> Option<Self::Item> where B: Ord, F: FnMut(&Self::Item) -> B:` Returns the element that gives the maximum value from the specified function

- `fn min_by_key<B, F>(self, f: F) -> Option<Self::Item> where B: Ord, F: FnMut(&Self::Item) -> B:` Returns the element that gives the minimum value from the specified function

- `fn rev(self) -> Rev<Self> where Self: DoubleEndedIterator:` Reverses an iterator's direction

- `fn unzip <A, B, FromA, FromB> (self) -> (FromA, FromB) where FromA: Default + Extend<A>, FromB: Default + Extend<B>, Self: Iterator<Item=(A, B)>:` Converts an iterator of pairs into a pair of containers

- `fn cloned<'a, T>(self) -> Cloned<Self> where Self: Iterator<Item=&'a T>, T: 'a + Clone:` Creates an iterator that clones all of its elements

- `fn cycle(self) -> Cycle<Self> where Self: Clone:` Repeats an iterator endlessly

- `fn sum<S>(self) -> S where S: Sum<Self::Item>:` Sums the elements of an iterator

- `fn product<P>(self) -> P where P: Product<Self::Item>:` Iterates over the entire iterator, multiplying all the elements

- `fn cmp<I>(self, other: I) -> Ordering where I: IntoIterator <Item=Self::Item>, Self::Item: Ord:` Compares the elements of this Iterator with those of another

- `fn partial_cmp<I>(self, other: I) -> Option<Ordering> where I: IntoIterator, Self::Item: PartialOrd<I::Item>:` Compares the elements of this Iterator with those of another

- `fn eq<I>(self, other: I) -> bool where I: IntoIterator, Self::Item: PartialEq<I::Item>:` Determines if the elements of this Iterator are equal to those of another

- `fn ne<I>(self, other: I) -> bool where I: IntoIterator, Self::Item: PartialEq<I::Item>`: Determines if the elements of this `Iterator` are unequal to those of another
- `fn lt<I>(self, other: I) -> bool where I: IntoIterator, Self::Item: PartialOrd<I::Item>`: Determines if the elements of this Iterator are less than those of another
- `fn le<I>(self, other: I) -> bool where I: IntoIterator, Self::Item: PartialOrd<I::Item>`: Determines if the elements of this Iterator are less than or equal to those of another
- `fn gt<I>(self, other: I) -> bool where I: IntoIterator, Self::Item: PartialOrd<I::Item>`: Determines if the elements of this Iterator are greater than those of another
- `fn ge<I>(self, other: I) -> bool where I: IntoIterator, Self::Item: PartialOrd<I::Item>`: Determines if the elements of this Iterator are greater than or equal to those of another

- `impl<I> DoubleEndedIterator for Box<I> where I: DoubleEndedIterator + ?Sized`
    - `fn next_back(&mut self) -> Option<I::Item>`: Removes and returns an element from the end of the iterator

- `impl <T> ExactSizeIterator for Box<I> where I: ExactSizeIterator + ?Sized`
    - `fn len(&self) -> usize`: Returns the exact number of times the iterator will iterate.

- `impl<T> Clone for Box<[T]> where T:Clone`
    - `fn clone(&self) -> Box<[T]>`: Returns a copy of the value
    - `fn clone_from(&mut self, source: &Self)`: Performs copy-assignment from source

- `impl<T> Borrow<T> for Box<T> where T:?Sized`
    - `fn borrow(&self) -> &T`: Immutably borrows from an owned value

- `impl<T> BorrowMut<T> for Box<T> where T:?Sized`
  - `fn borrow_mut(&mut self) -> &mut T`: Mutably borrows from an owned value

- `impl<T> AsRef<T> for Box<T> where T:?Sized`
  - `fn as_ref(&self) -> &T`: Performs the conversion

- `impl<T> AsMut for Box<T> where T:?Sized`
  - `fn as_mut(&mut self) -> &mut T`: Performs the conversion

- `impl<'a, E: Error + 'a> From<E> from Box<Error + 'a>`
  - `fn from(err: E) -> Box<Error + 'a>`: Performs the conversion

- `impl From<String> for Box<Error + Send + Sync>`
  - `fn from(err: String) -> Box<Error + Send + Sync>`: Performs the conversion

- `impl From<'a, 'b> From<&'b str> for Box<Error + Send + Sync + 'a>`
  - `fn from(err: &'b str) -> Box<Error + Send + Sync + 'a>`: Performs the conversion

- `impl<T: Error> Error for Box<T>`
  - `fn description(&self) -> &str`: Short description of the error
  - `fn cause(&self) -> Option<&Error>`: Lower-level cause of this error, if any

- `impl<R: Read + ?Sized> Read for Box<R>`
  - `fn read(&mut self, buf: &mut [u8]) -> Result<usize>`: Pulls some bytes from this source into the specified buffer, returning how many bytes were read
  - `fn read_to_end(&mut self, buf: &mut Vec<u8>) -> Result<usize>`: Reads all bytes until EOF in this source, placing them into `buf`
  - `fn read_to_string(&mut self, buf: &mut String) -> Result<usize>`: Reads all bytes until EOF in this source, placing them into `buf`
  - `fn read_exact(&mut self, buf: &mut [u8]) -> Result<()>`: Reads the exact number of bytes required to fill `buf`
  - `fn by_ref(&mut self) -> &mut Self where Self: Sized`: Creates a *by reference* adaptor for this instance of `Read`

- `fn bytes(self) -> Bytes<Self> where Self: Sized`: Transforms this `Read` instance to an Iterator over its bytes
- `fn chain<R: Read>(self, next: R) -> Chain<Self, R> where Self: Sized`: Creates an adaptor that will chain this stream with another
- `fn take(self, limit: u64) -> Take<Self> where Self: Sized`: Creates an adaptor that will read at most limit bytes from it

- `impl <W: Write + ?Sized> Write for Box<W>`
  - `fn write(&mut self, buf: &[u8]) -> Result<usize>`: Writes a buffer into this object, returning how many bytes were written
  - `fn flush(&mut self) -> Result<()>`: Flushes this output stream, ensuring that all intermediately buffered contents reach their destination
  - `fn write_all(&mut self, buf: &[u8]) -> Result<()>`: Attempts to write an entire buffer into this write
  - `fn write_fmt(&mut self, fmt: Arguments) -> Result<()>`: Writes a formatted string into this writer, returning any error encountered
  - `fn by_ref(&mut self) -> &mut Self where Self: Sized`: Creates a *by reference* adaptor for this instance of `Write`

- `impl<S: Seek + ?Sized> Seek for Box<S>`
  - `fn seek(&mut self, pos: SeekFrom) -> Result<u64>`: Seeks to an offset, in bytes, in a stream

- `impl<B: BufRead + ?Sized> BufRead for Box<B>`
  - `fn fill_buf(&mut self) -> Result<&[u8]>`: Fills the internal buffer of this object, returning the buffer contents
  - `fn consume(&mut self, amt: usize)`: Tells this buffer that amt bytes have been consumed from the buffer, so they should no longer be returned in calls to be read
  - `fn read_until(&mut self, byte: u8, buf: &mut Vec<u8>) -> Result<usize>`: Reads all bytes into `buf` until the delimiter byte is reached

- `fn read_line(&mut self, buf: &mut String) -> Result<usize>`: Reads all bytes until a newline (the 0 x A byte) is reached, and appends them to the provided buffer
- `fn split(self, byte: u8) -> Split<Self> where Self: Sized`: Returns an iterator over the contents of this reader split on the byte byte
- `fn lines(self) -> Lines<Self> where Self: Sized`: Returns an iterator over the lines of this reader

std::cell

Used in conjunction with shared mutable containers:

 For details on using `Cells`, `RefCell`, and both interior and external references, see `Chapter 11`, *Concurrency in Rust*.

- `Std::cell::BorrowError`: Returned by `RefCell::try_borrow`
- `impl Display for BorrowError`
    - `fn fmt(&self, f: &mut Formatter) -> Result<(), Error>`: Formats the value using the given formatter.
- `impl Debug for BorrowError`
    - `fn fmt(&self, f: &mut Formatter) -> Result<(), Error>`: Formats the value using the given formatter.
- `impl Error for BorrowError`
    - `fn description(&self) -> &str`: A short description of the error
    - `fn cause(&self) -> Option<&Error>`: The lower-level cause of this error, if any

- `std::cell::BorrowMutError`: Returned by `RefCell::try_borrow_mut`
- `impl Display for BorrowMutError`
    - `fn fmt(&self, f: &mut Formatter) -> Result<(), Error>`: Formats the value using the given formatter

- `impl Debug for BorrowMutError`
  - `fn fmt(&self, f: &mut Formatter) -> Result<(),` `Error>`: Formats the value using the given formatter
- `impl Error for BorrowMutError`
  - `fn description(&self) -> &str`: A short description of the error
  - `fn cause(&self) -> Option<&Error>`: The lower-level cause of this error, if any

- `std::cell::Cell`: A mutable memory location that admits only `Copy` data

Methods

- `impl<T> Cell<T> where T: Copy`
  - `fn new(value: T) -> Cell<T>`: Creates a new Cell containing the given value
  - `fn get(&self) -> T`: Returns a copy of the contained value
  - `fn set(&self, value: T)`: Sets the contained value
  - `fn as_ptr(&self) -> *mut T`: Returns a raw pointer to the underlying data in this cell
  - `fn get_mut(&mut self) -> &mut T`: Returns a mutable reference to the underlying data

Traits

- `impl<T> PartialEq<Cell<T>> for Cell<T> where T: Copy + PartialEq<T>`
  - `fn eq(&self, other: &Cell<T>) -> bool`: Tests for self and other values being equal, and is used by `==`
  - `fn ne(&self, other: &Rhs) -> bool`: Tests for `!=`
- `impl<T> Default for Cell<T> where T: Copy + Default`
  - `fn default() -> Cell<T>`: Creates a `Cell<T>`, with the `Default` value for T
- `impl<T> Clone for Cell<T> where T: Copy`
  - `fn clone(&self) -> Cell<T>`: Returns a copy of the value
  - `fn clone_from(&mut self, source: &Self)`: Performs copy-assignment from source

- `impl<T> From<T> for Cell<T> where T: Copy`
    - `fn from(t: T) -> Cell<T>`: Performs the conversion
- `impl<T> Ord for Cell<T> where T: Copy + Ord`
    - `fn cmp(&self, other: &Cell<T>) -> Ordering`: This method returns an `Ordering` between self and other
- `impl<T> Debug for Cell<T> where T: Copy + Debug`
    - `fn fmt(&self, f: &mut Formatter) -> Result<(), Error>`: Formats the value using the given formatter
- `impl<T> PartialOrd<Cell<T>> for Cell<T> where T: Copy + PartialOrd<T>`
    - `fn partial_cmp(&self, other: &Cell<T>) -> Option<Ordering>`: This method returns an ordering between self and other values if one exists
    - `fn lt(&self, other: &Cell<T>) -> bool`: This method tests less than (for self and other) and is used by the < operator
    - `fn le(&self, other: &Cell<T>) -> bool`: This method tests less than or equal to (for self and other) and is used by the <= operator
    - `fn gt(&self, other: &Cell<T>) -> bool`: This method tests greater than (for self and other) and is used by the > operator
    - `fn ge(&self, other: &Cell<T>) -> bool`: This method tests greater than or equal to (for self and other) and is used by the >= operator

- `Std::cell::Ref`: Wraps a borrowed reference to a value in a `RefCell` box

Methods

- `impl<'b, T> Ref<'b, T> where T: ?Sized`
    - `fn clone(orig: &Ref<'b, T>) -> Ref<'b, T>`: Copies a `Ref`. The `RefCell` is already immutably borrowed, so this cannot fail.
    - `fn map<U, F>(orig: Ref<'b, T>, f: F) -> Ref<'b, U> where F: FnOnce(&T) -> &U, U: ?Sized`: Makes a new `Ref` for a component of the borrowed data. The `RefCell` is already immutably borrowed, so this cannot fail.

Trait implementation

- `impl<'b, T> Debug for Ref<'b, T> where T: Debug + ?Sized`
    - `fn fmt(&self, f: &mut Formatter) -> Result<(), Error>`: Formats the value using the given formatter
- `impl<'b, T> Deref for Ref<'b, T> where T: ?Sized`
    - `fn deref(&self) -> &T`: The method is called to dereference a value
- `Std::cell::RefCell`: A mutable memory location with dynamically checked borrow rules

Methods

- `impl<T> RefCell<T>`
    - `fn new(value: T) -> RefCell<T>`: Creates a new `RefCell` containing a value
    - `fn into_inner(self) -> T`: Consumes the `RefCell`, returning the wrapped value.
- `impl<T> RefCell<T> where T: ?Sized`
    - `fn borrow(&self) -> Ref<T>`: Immutably borrows the wrapped value.
      The borrow lasts until the returned `Ref` exits scope. Multiple immutable borrows can be taken out at the same time. Throws a panic if the value is currently mutably borrowed.
    - `fn try_borrow(&self) -> Result<Ref<T>, BorrowError>`: Immutably borrows the wrapped value, returning an error if the value is currently mutably borrowed. The borrow lasts until the returned `Ref` exits scope. Multiple immutable borrows can be taken out at the same time.
    - `fn borrow_mut(&self) -> RefMut<T>`: Mutably borrows the wrapped value. The borrow lasts until the returned `RefMut` exits scope. The value cannot be borrowed while this borrow is active (throws a panic).
    - `fn try_borrow_mut(&self) -> Result<RefMut<T>, BorrowMutError>`: Mutably borrows the wrapped value, returning an error if the value is currently borrowed. The borrow lasts until the returned `RefMut` exits scope. The value cannot be borrowed while this borrow is active.

- fn as_ptr(&self) -> *mut T: Returns a raw pointer to the underlying data in this cell.
- fn get_mut(&mut self) -> &mut T: Returns a mutable reference to the underlying data.

Trait implementations

- impl<T> PartialEq<RefCell<T>> for RefCell<T> where T: PartialEq<T> + ?Sized
  - fn eq(&self, other: &RefCell<T>) -> bool: Tests for self and other values being equal, and is used by ==
  - fn ne(&self, other: &Rhs) -> bool: Tests for !=
- impl<T> Default for RefCell<T> where T: Default
  - fn default() -> RefCell<T>: Creates a RefCell<T>, with the Default value for T
- impl<T> Clone for RefCell<T> where T: Clone
  - fn clone(&self) -> RefCell<T>: Returns a copy of the value
  - fn clone_from(&mut self, source: &Self): Performs copy-assignment from source
- impl<T> From<T> for RefCell<T>
  - fn from(t: T) -> RefCell<T>: Performs the conversion
- impl<T> Ord for RefCell<T> where T: Ord + ?Sized
  - fn cmp(&self, other: &RefCell<T>) -> Ordering: Returns an Ordering between self and other
- impl<T> Debug for RefCell<T> where T: Debug + ?Sized
  - fn fmt(&self, f: &mut Formatter) -> Result<(), Error>: Formats the value using the given formatter
- impl<T> PartialOrd<RefCell<T>> for RefCell<T> where T: PartialOrd<T> + ?Sized
  - fn partial_cmp(&self, other: &RefCell<T>) -> Option<Ordering>: Returns an ordering between self and other values if one exists
  - fn lt(&self, other: &RefCell<T>) -> bool: Tests less than (for self and other) and is used by the < operator
  - fn le(&self, other: &RefCell<T>) -> bool: Tests less than or equal to (for self and other) and is used by the <= operator

- `fn gt(&self, other: &RefCell<T>) -> bool`: Tests greater than (for self and other) and is used by the > operator
- `fn ge(&self, other: &RefCell<T>) -> bool`: Tests greater than or equal to (for self and other) and is used by the >= operator

The code examples are in `Chapter 11`, *Concurrency in Rust*.

std::char

This module is used for the Structs, Traits, and Enum character types.

- **Structs**: `DecodeUtf16`, `DecodeUtf16Error`, `EscapeDefault`, `EscapeUnicode`, `ToLowercase`, and `ToUpperCase`.
- **Constants**: `Max` and `Replacement_Character`.
- **Functions**: `decode_utf16`, `from_digit`, `from_u32`, and `from_u32_unchecked`.

std::clone

This is for use with types that cannot be implicitly copied.

More complex types (such as strings) are not implicitly copyable. These types have to be made explicitly copyable using the `Clone` trait and clonable using the `clone` method.

Structs, Traits, and Enums: Trait `Clone`.

std::cmp

This module provides the ability to order and compare data.

This module defines both `PartialOrd` (overloads <. <=, >, and >=) and `PartialEq` traits (overloads == and !=).

Structs, Traits, and Enums: Enum `Ordering`, traits `Eq` (equality comparisons), `Ord` (total order), `PartialEq` (partial equality relations), `PartialOrd` (values that can be compared for a sort-order) .

std::collections

This covers the vectors, maps, sets, and binary heaps.

There are four main categories of collection, but for the majority of the time `Vec` and `HashMap` should be used.

The collection types are

- Sequences (`Vec`, `VecDeque`, `LinkedList` - if you're used to C#, these provide the functionality of `List<T>`)
- Maps (`HashMap`, `BTreeMap`. For C# users, these equate roughly to `Dictionary<T, U>`, and `Map`)
- Sets (`HashSet`, `BTreeSet`)
- BinaryHeap

Which collection should be used depends on what you want to do. Each will have a performance impact depending on what you're doing, though usually it's only `HashMap` that will give a negative impact.

Examples of use:

- `Vec`: Creates a collection of type `T` that can be resized; elements can be added to the end
- `VecDeque`: Creates a collection of type `T`, but with elements insertable at both ends; needs a queue or double-ended queue (deque)
- `LinkedList`: Used when you want a `Vec` or `VecDeque`, and to split and append lists
- `HashMap`: Creates a cached association of keys with values
- BTreeMap: Use with key-pair values where in general you want the largest and smallest key-pair values
- BinaryHeap: Stores elements, but only processes the biggest or most important ones when you want them

Each of these collections deals with its own memory handling. This is important as collections are able to allocate more space as required (and within the limitations of the hardware capacity of the machine they are running on).

Consider the following: I create a Vec<T> without setting a capacity. Let T be a structure. This is not an uncommon occurrence. I add a number of objects to the Vec, and each is then allocated on the heap. The heap expands, which is fine. I then delete a number of these objects. Rust then *repositions* the other members of the heap belonging to the Vec.

If I allocated space using with_capacity, then we have a maximum allocation available, which further helps with memory handling. We can help memory allocation further by using shrink_to_fit, which reduces the size of our Vec to fit the size required.

Iterators

Iterators are very useful and used in libraries. Primarily, an iterator is used in a for loop. Almost all collections provide three iterators: iter, iter_mut, and into_iter. Each of the iterator types performs a different function:

- iter: This provides an iterator of immutable references to all contents of the collection in the order that best suits the collection type.
- iter_mut: This provides an iterator of mutable references in the same order as iter.
- into_iter: This transforms the collection into an iterator. Very useful when the collection isn't needed, but its contents are. The into_iter iterator also includes the ability to extend a vector.

Structs: BTreeMap, BTreeSet, BinaryHeap, HashMap, HashSet, LinkedList, and VecDeque.

std::convert

This module is used for the conversion between types.

> When writing a library, implement From<T> and TryFrom<T> instead of Into<T> and TryInto<T> as the From forms provide greater flexibility.

- **Implementations**: As* (reference-to-reference conversions), Into (consume the value in the conversion), From (useful for value and reference conversion), `TryFrom`, and `TryInto` (similar to `From` and `Into`, allows for failure)

- **Structs, Traits, and Enums**: Traits `AsMut`, `AsRef`, `From`, and `Into`

std::default

This trait provides meaningful values for types.

Default provides default values for various primitive types. If a complex type is used, you will need to implement `Default`.

Structs, Traits, and Enums: Trait `Default`.

std:env

This module is used for dealing with process environment.

Provides a number of functions to obtain values from the current operating systems.

Structs, Traits, and Enums

- **Enum**: `VarError` (possible errors from the `env::var` method)
- **Structs**: `Args` (yields a `String` for each argument), `ArgOs` (yields an `OsString` for each argument), `JoinPathsError` (returns an error when the paths fail to join), `SplitPaths` (iterates over `PathBuf` for parsing an environment variable to platform-specific conventions), `Vars`, and `VarsOS` (iterates over a snapshot of the environment variables for a process)

std:error

This module is used for working with errors.

Structs, Traits, and Enums: Trait `Error` (base functionality for all errors)

std::f32

This module is used to deal with 32-bit floating point types.

This module provides basic math constants: `Digits`, `Epsilon`, `Infinity`, `Mantissa_Digits`, `Max` (largest finite `f32` value), `Max_10_Exp`, `Max_Exp`, `Min` (smallest finite `f32` value), `Min_10_Exp`, `Min_Exp`, `Min_Positive` (smallest possible normalized `f32` value), `NAN`, `Neg_Infinity`, and `Radix`.

std::f64

This module is used to deal with 64-bit floating point types.

This module provides basic math constants: `Digits`, `Epsilon`, `Infinity`, `Mantissa_Digits`, `Max` (largest finite `f64` value), `Max_10_Exp`, `Max_Exp`, `Min` (smallest finite `f64` value), `Min_10_Exp`, `Min_Exp`, `Min_Positive` (smallest possible normalized `f64` value), `NAN`, `Neg_Infinity`, and `Radix`.

std:ffi

FFI is Rust's method of interacting with non-Rust libraries. This trait provides a number of utilities for this purpose.

Structs, Traits, and Enums: Structs `CStr`, `CString` (representation of a borrowed C string and an owned C-compatible string respectively), `FromBytesWithNullError` (error returned from `CStr::from_bytes_with_nul`), `IntoStringError` (error returned from `CString::into_string` to indicate a UTF8 error during a conversion), `NulError` (returns an error from `CString::new` indicating a null byte was found in the provided vector), `OsStr`, and `OsString` (slices into OS strings).

std::fmt

This module is used for formatting and outputting strings.

 This module provides the `format!` macro for dealing with output. The macro is extremely powerful and very flexible, and provides a great deal of functionality.

Structs, Traits, and Enums

- **Structs**: `Arguments` (represents a safely precompiled version of a format string and arguments), `DebugList`, `DebugMap`, `DebugSet`, `DebugStruct`, `DebugTuple` (helps with `fmt::Debug` implementations), `Error` (an error type returned from formatting a message into a stream), and `Formatter` (represents both where to emit formatting strings and how to format them).
- **Traits**: `Binary`, `Debug`, `Display`, `LowerExp`, `LowerHex`, `Octal`, `Pointer`, `UpperExp`, `UpperHex`, and `Write` (provides collection of methods that are required to format a message into a stream).
- **Functions**: `format` (takes a precompiled format string with arguments and returns a formatted string) and `write` (takes an output stream, a precompiled format string and list of arguments. The arguments will be formatted according to the specified format string).

std::fs

This module is used when using the filesystem and manipulating files.

 This module provides a set of cross-platform methods to manipulate the filesystem the application is sitting on. If at all possible, avoid using the `remove_dir_all` function.

Structs, Traits, and Enums

- **Structs**: `DirBuilder` (used to create directories), `DirEntry` (returned by the `ReadDir` iterator), File (opens a file on the filesystem), `FileType` (represents a type of file with accessors to each file type), `Metadata` (information about the file), `OpenOptions` (options and flags used to configure how a file is opened), `Permissions` (file permissions on a file), and `ReadDir` (an iterator over the entries in a directory).
- **Functions**: `canonicalize` (returns the canonical form of a path), `copy` (copies files), `create_dir`, `create_dir_all` (recursively creates a directory and all parent components if missing), `hard_link` (creates a hard link on the file system), `metadata` (gets the metadata for a given path and file), `read_dir` (returns an iterator over the entries within a directory), `read_link` (reads a symbolic link returning the file it points to), `remove_dir` (removes an empty directory), `remove_dir_all` (removes a directory on a path recursively—on some operating systems this can completely delete your hard drive, so be careful!), `remove_file` (deletes a file), `rename` (renames a given file or directory), `set_permissions` (sets permissions on a given file or directory), and `symlink_metadata` (queries the metadata for a file without following any symlinks).

std::hash

This module is used to provide hashing support.

This module ensures that the easiest way to create a hash for a given type is to use `#[derive(Hash)]`.

Structs, Traits, and Enums

- **Structs**: `BuildHasherDefault` (implements `BuildHasher` for all Hasher types that also implement `Default`) and `SipHasher` (implementation of `SipHash`)
- **Traits**: `BuildHasher`, `Hash`, and `Hasher`

std::i8

This module defines the 8-bit integer type.

This module defines the `MAX` and `MIN` constants.

std::i16

This module defines the 16-bit integer type.

This module defines the `MAX` and `MIN` constants.

std::i32

This module defines the 32-bit integer type.

This module defines the MAX and MIN constants.

std::i64

This module is used for working with the 64-bit integer type.

This module defines the MAX and MIN constants.

std::io

This module provides a number of facilities for core input/output.

This module provides code Read and Write functionality for not only normal control, but also for various stream types (such as TCP and File). Access can be sequential or random. IO behavior also depends on the platform the application sits on, so testing is highly encouraged.

Structs, Traits, and Enums

- **Structs**: `BufReader` (adds buffering to any reader), `BufWriter` (buffers the writer output), `Bytes` (an iterator of values of a reader), `Chain` (chains two readers), `Cursor` (wraps another type and provides the Seek implementation), `Empty` (reader that is always at EOF), `Error` (error type for IO operations), `IntoInnerError` (error returned by `into_inner` that combines the error and buffered writer object, which may be recovered), `LineWriter` (wraps a writer and buffers into it), `Lines` (iterates over the lines of `BufRead`), `Repeat` (reader that continually returns a byte), `Sink` (writer that moves data to null), `Split` (an iterator over the contents of `BufRead` split at a point), `Stderr` (a handle for the process standard error stream), `StdErrLock` (locked ref. to `Stderr`), `Stdin` (standard input stream), `StdinLock` (locked ref. to `Stdin`), `Stdout` (global output stream), `StdoutLock` (locked ref. to `Stdout`), and `Take` (limits the bytes read from the reader).
- **Enums**: `ErrorKind` and `SeekFrom`.
- **Traits**: `BufRead` (buffered input read), `Read` (reads bytes from source), `Seek` (provides cursor that can be moved within the stream), and `Write`.
- **Functions**: `copy` (copies contents of reader to writer), `empty` (new handle to an empty reader), `repeat` (creates an instance of reader that repeats 1 byte forever), `sink` (an instance of the writer that consumes all data), `stderr` (a new handle to `stderr`), `stdin` (a new handle to `stdin`), and `stdout` (a new handle to `stdout`).

std::isize

This module is for use with the pointer-sized integer type.

 This module defines the `MAX` and `MIN` constants.

std::iter

This module is used for iteration.

Structs, Traits, and Enums

- **Structs**: Chain (strings two iterators together), Cloned (clones the underlying iterator), Cycle (never-ending iterator), Empty (yields nothing), Enumerate (yields the current count and element while iterating), Filter (filters the elements of iter with predicate), FilterMap (iterator that uses a type for both filter and map from iter), FlatMap (maps each element to the iterator, yields the elements produced), Fuse (yields None continually once the underlying iterator first iterates None), Inspect (calls a function with a reference to each element before yielding it), Map (maps the values of iter with a type), Once (yields an element once), Peekable (allows peek() to be used), Repeat (repeats an element forever), Rev (double ended iterator with the read direction reversed), Scan (maintains state while iterating another iterator), Skip (skips *n* elements of iter), SkipWhile (rejects elements while predicate is true), Take (only iterates over the first *n* of iter), TakeWhile (only accepts elements to iterate over while the predicate is true), and Zip (iterates two iterators simultaneously).
- **Traits**: DoubleEndedIterator (yields the elements at both ends), ExactSizeIterator (exact length known), Extend (extends a collection with the contents of an iterator), FromIterator (converts from Iterator), ToIterator (converts into Iterator), and Iterator (interface for dealing with iterators).
- **Functions**: empty (new iterator that yields nothing), once (new iterator that yields an element once), and repeat (new iterator that continually repeats a single element).

std::marker

This module provides primitive traits and markers to represent basic kinds of type.

Structs, Traits, and Enums

- **Struct**: `PhantomData` (allows the description of type `T`).
- **Traits**: `Copy` (types that can be copied), `Send` (types that can be transferred across threads), `Sized` (types with a constant size), and `Sync` (types that can be safely shared between threads).

std::mem

This module performs memory handling functions.

 This module is used to query size and alignment types, initialization, and the manipulation of memory.

Structs, Traits, and Enums

- **Functions**: `align_of` (returns alignment in memory of type), `align_of_val` (minimum alignment of type of value `val` points to), `drop` (disposes), `forget` (leaves a value to void, takes ownership but doesn't run the destructor), `replace` (replaces the value at a `mut` location with a new one, returns the old value but doesn't de-initialize or copy either one), `size_of` (returns size of type in bytes), `size_of_val` (returns the size of a value in bytes), `swap` (swaps the values of two `mut` locations; must be of the same type), `transmute` (unsafely transforms a value of one type into another), `transmute_copy` (interprets `src` as `&T`, then reads `src` without moving the contained value), `uninitialized` (bypasses Rust's memory initialization requirement), and `zeroed` (creates a value initialized to zero).

std:net

This module provides basic TCP/UDP communication primitives.

Structs, Traits, and Enums

- **Structs**: AddrParseError (error returned when parsing an IP or socket address), Incoming (infinite iterator over connections from TcpListener), Ipv4Addr (represents an IPv4 address), Ipv6Addr (represents an IPv6 address), SocketAddrV4 (IPv4 socket address), SocketAddrV6 (IPv6 socket address), TcpListener (represents a socket server), TcpStream (represents a TCP stream between the local and remote sockets), and UdpSocket (UDP socket).
- **Enums**: IpAddr (either an IPv4 or IPv6 address), Shutdown (values passed to the shutdown method of TcpStream), and SocketAddr (socket address for networking applications).
- **Trait**: ToSocketAddrs (object that can be converted to or resolved from one or more SocketAddr values).

std::num

This module is used for dealing with numbers.

This module provides extra types that are useful for dealing with numbers.

Structs, Traits, and Enums

- **Structs**: ParseFloatError (error returned when parsing a float), ParseIntError (error returned when parsing an int), and Wrapping (intentionally-wrapped arithmetic on T).
- **Enum**: FpCategory (classification of floating point numbers).

std::os

This module contains functions that provide abstracted access to the OS the application is running on.

This module contains three modules: `linux` (Linux-specific), `raw` (raw OS-specific types for current platform), and `unix` (experimental extension).

std::panic

This module provides support for panic within the standard library.

Structs, Traits, and Enums

- **Structs**: `AssertUnwindSafe` (checks whether a type is panic-safe), `Location` (information about the panic location), and `PanicInfo` (information about the panic).
- **Traits**: `RefUnwindSafe` (trait that represents types where the shared ref is considered `recovery` safe) and `UnwindSafe` (trait that represents panic-safe types in Rust).
- **Functions**: `catch_unwind` (invokes a closure, captures the cause of the unwind), `resume_unwind` (triggers a panic without invoking the panic), `set_hook` (registers a custom panic hook and replaces previous hooks), and `take_hook` (unregisters a current panic hook).

std::path

This module provides abstracted access to the path in a cross-platform way for manipulation.

Two types are provided, `PathBuf` and `Path`. These are wrappers around `OsString` and `OsStr` and allow direct work to be performed on strings according to the local platform path.

Structs, Traits, and Enums

- **Structs**: Components (core iterator giving the parts of a path), Display (for safely printing paths with format!() and {}), Iter (iterator over the parts of a path), Path (slice of a path), PathBuf (owned mutable path), PrefixComponent (Windows-specific path prefix), and StripPrefixError (error returned from the Path::strip_prefix method indicating the prefix was not found in self).
- **Enums**: Component (single component of a path) and Prefix (path prefix [Windows only]).
- **Function**: is_separator (determines whether the character is one of the permitted path separators).

std::process

This module is used for working with processes.

Structs, Traits, and Enums

- **Structs**: Child (represents a running or exited child process), ChildStderr (handle to a child process stderr), ChildStdin (handle child process stdin), ChildStdout (handle for child process stdout), Command (acts as a process builder), ExitStatus (describes the result of a process after it is terminated), Output (output of finished process), and Stdio (describes what to do with the standard IO stream for a child process).
- **Function**: exit (terminates current process with exit code).

std::ptr

This module provides access for handling raw, unsafe pointers.

 See Chapter 5, *Remember, Remember*, for more details.

Structs, Traits, and Enums

Functions: copy (copies `count * size_of<T>` from `src` to `dest`; can overlap), `copy_nonoverlapping` (same as `copy`, except cannot overlap), `drop_in_place` (executes destructor of the pointed-to value), `null` (new null raw pointer), `null_mut` (new null mutable raw pointer), `read` (reads value from `src` without moving it), `read_volatile` (volatile read of the value from `src` without moving it), `replace` (replaces value at `dest` with `src`, returning the old value), `swap` (swaps the values at two mutable locations of the same type), `write` (overwrites the memory location with the value without reading or dropping the old value), `write_bytes` (invokes `memset` on the specified pointer), and `write_volatile` (performs a volatile write of a memory location with a given value).

std::slice

This module provides a dynamically-sized placement into a contiguous `[T]`.

Slices are mutable (`&mut [T]`) or shared slices (`&[T]`) of memory represented as a pointer. They implement `IntoIter`, which duplicates the type `IntoIter` is being performed on.

Structs, Traits, and Enums

- **Structs**: `Chunks` (iterates over a non-overlapping slice in chunks of `size_of<T>` elements at a time), `ChunksMut` (as for `Chunks` except are mutable), `Iter` (immutable iterator), `IterMut` (mutable iterator), `RSplitN` and `RSplitNMut` (iterate over sub-slices that match a predicate, limited to a given number of splits, and start from the end of the slice). `Split` and `SplitMut` (iterator over sub-slice separated by elements that match a predicate function or predicate respectively), and `SplitN` and `SplitNMut` (iterate over sub-slices that match predicate function), and `Windows` (iterates over overlapping sub-slice of length `size_of<T>`).
- **Functions**: `from_raw_parts` (forms a slice from a pointer and length) and `from_raw_parts_mut` (as `from_raw_parts` except the slice returned is mutable).

std::str

This module is used for Unicode string slices.

Structs, Traits, and Enums

- **Structs**: Bytes (iterator for a strings bytes), CharIndices (iterator for a string's characters and byte offsets), Chars (iterator for the char of a string), EncodeUtf16 (external iterator for a string's UTF16 code), Lines (created with lines()), MatchIndices (created with match_indices()), Matches (created with matches()), ParseBoolError (error returned when passing a bool from a string fail), RMatchIndicies (created with rmatch_indicies()), RMatches (created with rmatches()), RSplit (created with rsplit()), RSplitN (created with rsplitn()), RSplitTerminator (created with rsplit_terminator()), Split (created with split()), SplitN (created with splitn()), SplitTerminator (created with split_terminator()), SplitWhitespace (iterates over the non-whitespace substrings of a string), and Utf8Error (error that can occur when attempting to interpret a sequence of u8 as a string)
- **Trait**: FromStr (abstracts the idea of creating a new instance of a type from a string)
- **Functions**: from_utf8 (converts a slice of bytes to a string slice) and from_utf8_unchecked (as with from_utf8 without checking the string contains valid UTF8)

std::string

This module provides string handling with a UTF-8 encoded growable string.

Contains the String type and a trait to convert to a String (ToString) as well as error types.

Structs, Traits, and Enums

- **Structs**: Drain (draining iterator), FromUtf16Error (possible error value when converting from a UTF16 slice), and FromUtf8Error (as for FromUtf16Error except for UTF8), and String (UTF8-encoded growing string).
- **Enum**: ParseError.
- **Trait**: ToString (converts a value to a string).

std::sync

This module provides thread synchronization functions.

This is covered in Chapter 11, *Concurrency in Rust*.

Structs, Traits, and Enums

- **Structs**: Arc (atomic ref counted wrapper), Barrier (enables multiple threads to synchronize the beginning of some computation), BarrierWaitResult (result from a thread wait), Condvar (CONDitional VARiable), Mutex (mutual exclusion primitive), MutexGuard (scoped lock mutex; becomes unlocked when the structure goes out of scope), Once (sync primitive used to run a one-time global initialization), PoisonError (error that can be returned when a lock is required), RwLock (read/write lock), RWLockReadGuard (used to release shared read access to a lock when dropped), RWWriteGuard (used to release shared write access if a lock when dropped), WaitTimeoutResult (type used to determine whether a condition variable timed out or not), and Weak (weak pointer to Arc).
- **Enum**: TryLockError (errors that may occur when calling try_lock).

See the code examples in Chapter 11, *Concurrency in Rust*.

std::thread

This is the main threading module, providing native threads to your Rust application.

 Threading is covered in `Chapter 11`, *Concurrency in Rust*.

Structs, Traits, and Enums

- **Structs**: `Builder` (provides detailed control over new threads), `JoinHandle` (owned permission to join on a thread), `LocalKey` (key to local storage that owns the contents), and `Thread` (handle to thread).
- **Functions**: `current` (get handle to the thread invocation), `panicking` (if the thread is unwinding due to a panic), `park` (blocks unless or until the token is available), `park_timeout` (blocks for a duration), and `sleep` (puts the current thread to sleep for a duration), `spawn` (spawns a new thread, returns a `JoinHandle`), and `yield_now` (gives up a timeslice to the OS scheduler).

 See the code examples in `Chapter 11`, *Concurrency in Rust*.

std::time

This is a module for handling time.

Structs, Traits, and Enums

Structs: `Duration` (represents a span of time), `Instant` (measurement of a monotonically increasing clock), `SystemTime` (measures the system clock), and `SystemTimeError` (error returned from `SystemTime.duration_since()`).

std::u8

This module defines the unsigned 8-bit integer type.

This module defines the MAX and MIN constants.

std::u16

This module defines the unsigned 16-integer type.

This module defines the MAX and MIN constants.

std::u32

This module defines the unsigned 32-bit integer type.

This module defines the MAX and MIN constants.

std::u64

This module defines the unsigned 64-bit integer type.

This module defines the MAX and MIN constants.

std::usize

This is the pointer-sized unsigned integer type.

 This module defines the MAX and MIN constants.

std::vec

This module defines the growable array type with heap-allocated contents.

 This is written as Vec<T>, and values are added to (or removed from) the end of the vec using push and pull, respectively.

Structs, Traits, and Enums

Structs: Drain (draining iterator for Vec<T>), IntoIter (iterator that moves out of a vector), and Vec (contiguous growable array type).

Summary

We have covered a sizable portion of the Rust standard library. Always check the official documentation online at https://doc.rust-lang.org/std/—it is of an exceptionally high quality and always up-to-date!

In the next and last chapter, we will take a look at using external libraries from Rust via its **Foreign Function Interface (FFI)**.

14
Foreign Function Interfaces

Given that Rust is a language primarily designed to work on servers and most libraries sitting on a server aren't written in Rust (yet!), it makes sense that Rust applications should be able to utilize libraries written in other languages. In this chapter, we will be examining how to do this.

Specifically, we will cover the following:

- Learning how we can utilize other libraries
- Understanding the pitfalls of using code written in another language
- Ensuring, as far as is practicable, that our code will remain safe

As with previous chapters, the source code will be available for you to examine. You will also find a small library written in C to compile for Windows, macOS, and Linux. The library doesn't do very much but gives you an understanding of how the system works. Other libraries (such as `ImageMagick`) work in exactly the same way.

Let's make a start!

Introducing our simple library

Libraries come in three flavors: `.dll` (dynamic linkable library) for Windows, `.so` (shared object), and `.a`—`.a` and `.so` are typically found on Unix type systems (including macOS).

Our library is very simple; it acts as a calculation library—you pass in the values to the correct function and the result is returned. Not rocket science but enough to prove what we're going to do.

When using external libraries, we will need to use the `unsafe` directive. Rust cannot control what an external library delivers and therefore if we used standard code, the compiler will not allow compilation.

As developers, using external libraries must be handled with care.

The three-step program

There are essentially three steps to using a library within your Rust application:

1. Including the dependency.
2. Writing code that uses the library.
3. Building your application to link to the library.

The most difficult stage is the second as it requires writing code, call back code, and other such wrappers to use the library.

Including the dependency

As with using any library not provided by `Prelude`, the compiler has to know of the existence of the library. As we did in Chapter 8, *The Rust Application Lifetime*, we let the compiler know to expect an external library by including in the `Cargo.toml` file, as follows:

```
[dependency]
libc = "0.2.0"
```

The figure in quotes is the library version. This is useful to have in as it enables the compiled Rust application to only run against a particular version of the library, which guarantees the code required will be in the library. The downside is that in order to always ensure the library is available, the compiled binary will need to ship with that library. In this case (and this is the case for most external libraries), `libc` will need to be added.

We also need to include the following line to the source file where the functions will be called:

```
extern crate libc;
```

Creating the code

The code for this part is in `Chapter 14/firstexample`.

When we are dealing with code from outside our application, we need to be able to tell the compiler something akin to "*Hey look, build this code and just leave a hook to something that may or may not exist and that may or may not take these parameters but that will return something hopefully.*" It's like handing a blank check to a fraudster with your signature on and hoping they won't write something in and cash it!

In Rust, we do this by using the link directive and enclosing the function in an `extern` block. The code inside the `extern` calls the function held within the library. It must be the same as the name of the function within the library:

```
[link(name="mathlib")]
extern
  {
      fn add_two_int_numbers(a: i32, b: i32) -> i32;
  }
```

This code is then accessed using the following:

```
fn main()
  {
     let ans = unsafe { add_two_int_numbers(10,20) };
     println!("10 + 20 = {}", ans);
  }
```

What's the [link(name="")] for?

This is a directive that tells the compiler that the code is going to link to a library called whatever is inside the quotes. You don't need the likes of `mathlib.dll`, `mathlib.so`, or `mathlib.a` inside the quotes, just the name without the extension.

There are three different types of link (called models and defined in the `kind` parameter following the **name**) available: *dynamic*, *static*, and *framework* (though the latter is for macOS only). The following table gives a summary of what they are for. For the majority of the time, the `dynamic` type is used.

Type	Example	Notes
Dynamic	`[link(name="foo")]`	This is the default. The compiled binary creates *hooks* that will link into the platform installed form of the library.
Static	`[link(name="foo", kind="static")]`	These are `.a` files. When the application is built, the binary is created, but the platform library file is not required to be distributed.
Framework	`[link(name="foo", kind="framework")]`	macOS only. This will be the `.dylib` file and is treated the same as a dynamic library.

What's the big deal? That was simple enough!

While on the face of it, using an external library via FFI is not rocket science, it does come with a number of issues. Why do we need to annotate blocks with unsafe even when we are referring to known names in libraries?

As we have seen time and again with Rust, the compiler does an awful lot for the developer that you won't see in many other compilers. It ensures thread safety, that a particular operation can be achieved, the buffers don't overrun, that we don't leave memory unallocated or attempt to deallocate twice, and plenty of other things that ensure that, as far as possible, the code we have will run and remain rock-solid (in terms of reliability).

Unfortunately, with external libraries, all the compiler can do is to expect something from a linked library. Threads may be left hanging or be plain unsafe; there is no guarantee that if I passed in 6 and 0 for a similar division function, what is returned is a number and pretty much anything else can go wrong.

By using `unsafe`, we give the compiler a promise that when it links the code, what it links to will be bound correctly.

Let's extend things a bit

The `extern` block can include as many (or as few) of the methods required from the library the Rust application is using.

> With each new function added to the `extern` block, it is always a good idea to test the function being included. This can be done as either unit tests or by adding the function to the `extern` block and then calling that function from within `main`.

We can also have multiple Rust source files that include the library functions.

For example, make the changes in the `Source1.rs` file:

```
//Source1.rs
[link(name="mylib")]
extern
{
    fn some_method(a: f32) → f32;
    fn some_other_method(a: i32, b: f32, c: f64) → f64;
}
```

Now, make changes in the `Source2.rs` file:

```
[link(name="mylib")]
extern
 {
    fn some_other_method(a: i32, b: f32, c: f64) → f64;
    fn some_text_method() → String;
}
```

As long as the link line is included, this won't cause an issue.

What happens if the types don't match?

There is no guarantee that when you build a library on a 32-bit platform, an `int` will have the same `size_t` as an `int` on a 64-bit platform. They usually will, but there is no guarantee. A simple example is this:

```
sizeof(char) == 1
sizeof(short) <= sizeof(int) <= sizeof(long) <= sizeof(long long)
```

Therefore, a short can be the same size as a long! More usually, though, `int` will be the platform word size (32 bits on a 32-bit processor, 64 bits on a 64-bit processor).

Values for floats are stricter and comply with the IEEE 754 standards.

There is not normally an issue if the Rust application is built on a 64-bit platform and the library is 32 bits. If it is the other way around, however, there is a chance that an overflow may occur. It is unlikely, but worth keeping in mind.

Can we make things safer?

There is a strategy that we can take to try and make things slightly safer.

Consider our original `extern` code:

```
[link(name="mathlib")]
extern
 {
     fn add_two_int_numbers(a: i32, b: i32) -> i32;
 }
```

This code is calling a raw C API and, as discussed, any calls to this have to be marked as being `unsafe`. It is unsafe as the call is known as being **low level**.

In terms of programming languages, the lower the language, the closer it is to being a language understood by the processor (an assembler is considered the lowest language that is of any real use, short of poking raw binary into a memory location). Here we are exposing the library at its lowest level.

In order to make the call safer, we use something known as **wrapping**.

Wrappers

Wrappers are very common when using a library designed for another language. They work by exposing a higher-level function name that *hides* the true method working underneath. The exposed function name is commonly known as the library interface API. By only exposing the higher-level function name, Rust is able to keep the unsafe part away from the rest of the world.

A practical example

One of the methods in the library takes a vector of int values to perform a mean, median, and mode calculation, which in turn returns an array of float values containing these values. However, we need to validate the values first (essentially, test the array is not empty) and that there are five or more values. This will return a boolean.

The unsafe version of the code would be:

```
[link(name="mathlib")]
extern
  {
      fn check_mean_mode_median(a: Vec<i32>) -> bool;
  }
```

We can create a wrapper for this quite simply:

```
pub fn calc_mean_mode_median_check(a:Vec<int32>) -> bool
  {
     unsafe
  {
         check_mean_mode_median(a) == 0;
     }
  }
```

We expose the safe function to the code and hide (wrap) the unsafe part. Once we have a value of true returned, we know the data is safe to have the calculation.

Now, this is a pretty pointless piece of code (it is simply a test to ensure we have the right number of parameters in the vector). Let's modify this wrapper so that we return a Vec<f32>, which will contain $-999f$, $-999f$, or $-999f$ if the check fails, or mean, median and mode of the values of the vector.

The issue though is that the original library is in C, so we need to get the results as an array and then put that into a vector.

The first part is making the first check:

```
pub fn mean_mode_median(a: Vec<int32>) -> Vec<f32>
  {
     // we can have this result outside of the unsafe as it is a guaranteed
parameter
     // it must be mutable as it is used to store the result if the result
is returned
     let mut result = vec![-999f32, -999f32, -999f32];
     unsafe
  {
```

```
            if check_mean_mode_median(a) != 0
    {
                return result;
        }
    else
    {
                let res = calc_mean_median_mode(a);
    result = res.to_vec();
                return result;
        }
    }
}
```

Not only do we now have a single call to the external library, but we also have guarantees the compiler needs.

Accessing global variables

Quite frequently within a C library, there will be global variables that are used for such things as version details and build-specific code. Rust can access these in a similar way to other variables:

```
extern crate libc;
#[link(name = "mathlib")]
extern {
    static code_version: libc::c_int;
}
fn main() {
    println!("You have mathlib version {} installed.", code_version as
i32);
}
```

Cleaning up after yourself

While the maths library is a very simple example, there may be times when you need to use a library that passes back a large block of data (such as you would expect if you created a wrapper to work with ImageMagick—a commonly used and extremely capable graphics library). When the library returns, the results are passed off to the Rust application, which you will need to deallocate manually.

To help you with this, Rust provides the Drop trait.

Drop it!

The Drop trait is a very simple trait:

```
pub trait Drop
{
    fn drop(&mut self);
}
```

As with all traits, it requires an impl for it before the trait can be used:

```
struct FreeMemory;
impl Drop for FreeMemory
{
    fn drop(&mut self);
}
```

At this point, we call our pub fn, which returns a data block from ImageMagick. Once we have done what we need to do with that memory block, we have to free it. We stored the data in a variable called graphics_block. To free the block from graphics_block, we use:

```
graphics_block  = FreeMemory;
```

The memory is freed once graphics_block goes out of scope.

> It is worth pointing out that panic! will call drop as it unwinds the memory. If you therefore have a panic! within a drop, chances are that it is going to abort.

Monitoring an external process within an FFI

During your time using a computer, you will have no doubt seen an image like the following:

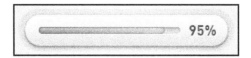

These progress bars work in a similar way to each other. Say you have a process that has five equal sized portions or you're downloading a file from the internet. As the portion completes or an amount of code is downloaded, the bar and percentage are updated using a programming technique known as a **callback**.

How a callback is implemented depends on the language being used. For example, in an event-driven language, the process will either emit a signal or generate an event that the receiver listens for. When the signal/event is received, the user interface is updated.

Rust is no different; it is able to use a callback when using an FFI. Rust is capable of working with both synchronous and asynchronous callbacks. It is also possible to target a callback to a Rust object.

Targeting synchronous callbacks

Synchronous callbacks are the simplest to target, as they are normally always on the same thread. Therefore, we don't have to deal with the code being more unsafe than usual, which is normally the case with asynchronous callbacks.

 The code for this part is in `Chapter 14/synccallback`. Instructions for building on Linux, macOS, and Windows are included in the source examples.

Let's deal with the Rust side of the code first. Here, we have three parts:

1. The function for the callback itself:

```
extern fn my_callback(percent: i32)
{
    println!("Process is now {}% complete", percent);
}
```

2. The calls to the external code:

```
[link(name="external_lib")]
extern
{
    fn register_callback(call: extern fn(i32)) -> i32;
    fn do_callback_trigger();
}
```

3. Fire off the code:

```
fn main()
 {
    unsafe
 {
        register_callback(my_callback);
        do_callback_trigger();
    }
 }
```

`register_callback(my_callback)` and `fn register_callback(call: extern fn(i32))` `->→` `i32;` may look strange at first glance. In a normal function call, the parameters within the braces are passed into the receiving function, which then does something with them.

Here, we are passing a function as the parameter, which we really can't do (or at least shouldn't). Callbacks though are different, as the function is by virtue of the `extern` modifier counted as a pointer that takes the returned value from the external library as its own parameter.

Targeting a Rust object

In the last example, we had a callback that listened for a single `int`. What happens though if we want to listen out for a complex object from the external library (for example, a structure)? We can't return a structure, but we can have a Rust object that can be mapped to the callback.

It is a slightly more complex affair than for a synchronous callback:

1. Create the structure that will map to the external structure we're interested in:

```
#[repr(C)] // this is a name used within the extern in (2)
struct MyObject
 {
    a: i32,
    // and anything else you want to get back from the library
    // just make sure you add them into the call back
 }
```

2. Create the callback; `result` is a pointer to the mutable `myobject`:

```
extern "C" fn callback(result: *mut MyObject, a: i32)
{
    unsafe
    {
        (*result).a = a;
    }
}
```

3. Create the `extern` functions to the library:

```
#[link(name="external_lib")]
extern
{
    fn register_callback(result: mut MyObject, cback: extern fn(mut
MyObject, i32));
    fn start_callback();
}
```

4. Create the calling code:

```
fn main()
{
    // we need to create an object for the callback
    let mystruct = Box::new (MyObject{a: 5i32});
    unsafe {
        register_callback(&mut *mystruct, callback);
        start_callback();
    }
}
```

Calling Rust from another language

Rust can also be called from a different language and it's a simple process. The only caveat is that the name used has to be unmangled. If you recall from Chapter 8, *The Rust Application Lifetime*, when you use a generic, the compiler generates the necessary code to ensure the linker works. It does this by mangling the names to ensure that the correct code is compiled and called when the code needs it.

Unmangling is the opposite of this; it preserves the name of the function in use:

```
#[no_mangle]
pub extern fn hello_world() -> *const u8 {
    "Hello, world!\0".as_ptr()
}
```

This can then be called from within your own (non-Rust) application.

Dealing with the unknown

C developers don't always pass parameters between functions that have *strong* types; rather, they pass a void* type. This is then cast to be something solid within the receiving function. In a way, this is very similar to passing a generic type between functions.

These have to be dealt with in a different way if you want to access a function within a library that has a void* as a parameter type.

For example, the C functions may be:

```
void output_data(void *data);
void transformed_data(void *data);
```

As we don't have anything in Rust the same as void*, we need to use a mutable pointer:

```
extern crate libc;
extern "C"
  {
    pub fn output_data(arg: *mut libc::c_void);
    pub fn transformed_data(arg: *mut libc::c_void);
}
```

This will do the job.

C structs

Earlier in this chapter, we used a struct as a parameter. In C, there is nothing to stop the developer passing a structure as a parameter:

```
struct MyStruct;
struct MyOtherStruct;
void pass_struct(struct MyStruct *arg);
void pass_struct2(struct MyOtherStruct *arg2);
```

`MyStruct` and `MyOtherStruct` are known as opaque structs. The name is exposed, but the private parts aren't.

Handling a `struct` within Rust is not as simple as you'd first think, but then it's not that difficult either. The only difference is that we use an empty `enum` instead of a `struct` when interfacing with the C library. This creates our opaque type that stores the information from the C opaque type. As the `enum` is empty, we can't instantiate it and, more importantly, as `MyStruct` and `MyOtherStruct` aren't the same, we have type-safety and so can't get them mixed up:

```
enum MyStruct {};
enum MyOtherStruct {};
extern "C"
{
    pub fn pass_struct(arg: *mut MyStruct);
    pub fn pass_struct2(arg: *mut MyOtherStruct);
}
```

Summary

We have covered something in this chapter that not only makes Rust an excellent choice for developing applications with, but by using libraries that aren't Rust ones, also makes it a flexible and powerful language. There are pitfalls (such as needing to use unsafe and having to be very careful with panic! code), but there are far more advantages than downfalls.

For the purposes of this text, `.dll` is purely for Windows. The .NET Framework also uses `.dll` files that, if they don't include anything Windows-specific, can also be used on macOS and Linux.

Index

www.ingramcontent.com/pod-product-compliance
Lightning Source LLC
LaVergne TN
LVHW081517050326
832903LV00025B/1528